Three Lectures on Post-Industrial Society

Three Lectures on Post-Industrial Society

Daniel Cohen

translated by William McCuaig

The MIT Press
Cambridge, Massachusetts
London, England

For information on quantity discounts, email special_sales@mitpress.mit.edu.

Set in Palatino by The MIT Press. Printed and bound in the United States of America.

Library of Congress Cataloging-in-Publication Data

Cohen, Daniel, 1953–
[Trois legons sur la sociiti post-industrielle. English]
Three lectures on post-industrial society / Daniel Cohen; translated by William McCuaig.
    p.   cm.
Previously published in French as: Trois legons sur la sociiti post-industrielle.
Includes bibliographical references and index.
ISBN 978-0-262-03383-1 (hbk.: alk. paper)
    1. Globalization—Economic aspects.   2. Globalization—Social aspects.
3. Social history—21st century.   4. Europe—Social policy.   I. McCuaig, William, 1949–   II. Title.
HF1359.C65213   2008
330.9—dc22   2008017004

10 9 8 7 6 5 4 3 2 1

to the three Suzies

Contents

Acknowledgements

The three chapters in this book are adapted from three lectures given at the Collège de France in the "Grand Angle-Altadis" cycle. I thank Olivier Mongin for the invitation and Kemal Dervis, Mario Monti, Josep Ramoneda, and Pierre Rosanvallon for their stimulating commentary. Friendly thoughts as well for Perrine Simon-Nahum, the publisher of my previous books, and Isabelle Albaret, who organized the lectures.

Three Lectures on
Post-Industrial
Society

Introduction

Marx thought that history moved through phases, and that capitalism was only one of them. Today we are discovering that capitalism itself has a history, that it manifests itself differently in the twentieth century than it did in the nineteenth, and that today it is unlike what it was yesterday.

The capitalism of the twentieth century was constructed around a central figure: the industrial firm.[1] The firm established what the French sociologist Emile Durkheim might have called an organic solidarity among its members. The engineers concentrated on making the unskilled workers productive, and the managers were salary earners themselves, with the same ultimate goal as their employees: to shield the firm from the hazards of the economic environment. Huge conglomerates were created to reduce industry risk; for example, a firm that made bathing suits would attempt to acquire an umbrella maker as a hedge against climatic unpredictability, so that, whatever the weather, its workers would still have jobs. Mirroring feudal society, the industrial society of the twentieth century linked a mode of production to a mode of protection. It bonded the economic question to the social question.

Twenty-first-century capitalism is engaged in systematically dismantling that industrial society. The various levels of large industrial enterprises are being uncoupled from one another. Tasks not considered essential are now assigned to subcontractors. The engineers are grouped together in independent research bureaus, where they never come across workers. The employees in charge of the cleaning, of the cafeteria, and of the day-care facilities are recruited by specialized companies. The financial revolution of the 1980s changed the principles on which firms organize. From the shareholder's point of view, there is no need for the same company to make bathing suits and umbrellas; the shareholder can spread his risk by owning a share of a company making each. In a Copernican-like reversal of the very foundations of the wage-earning class, workers are being exposed to rising uncertainty about their incomes while shareholders are shielding themselves against uncertainty.[2] The solidarity that was at the heart of the industrial firm has disappeared.

The Service Society

To speak of post-industrial society as a way of characterizing these transformations is to speak a bit loosely. It is to describe the world by what it no longer is (the industrial society) rather than by what is has become. If we want to define the current transformation more affirmatively, we have several options. One is to call this a shift to a service society, using the classification into primary (agriculture), secondary (industry), and tertiary (service) sectors. The British economist Colin Clark as early as 1939, and the French economist Jean Fourastié in 1946, heralded the coming of a service society. Fourastié saw the world of the future as one in which man would finally be set free from working the soil in rural societies, or raw materials in industrial societies.[3] With the coming of a service society, the material worked by man is man himself. Whether a hairdresser or a doctor, the worker reconnects directly with other people. Economists have coined a term that reflects this notion: *face to face* (abbreviated F2F), meaning work that demands direct contact between the producer and the client.

A lot of water has passed under the bridge since the publication of Fourastié's book. In terms of strict tabulation, there is no doubt that employment has shifted from industry to services, just as it shifted from agriculture into industry a century earlier. In October 2005 the British magazine *The Economist* published an article indicating that the proportion of industrial employment in the United States had fallen below 10 percent. Seeking as always to highlight paradoxical notions, *The Economist* added that this already low figure actually understated the reality of shrinkage. Within the industrial sector, an

increasing share of the work involves conception and
marketing. Industry itself is becoming a service-intensive
sector. The number of workers carrying out strictly industrial tasks—tasks that consist of fabricating, by hand or
with the help of a robot, a "manufactured" product—
might even be less than half the stated figure. Soon such
workers may be no more numerous than farmers.

But there is a risk of misunderstanding here. The tertiarized economy has not in the least "got rid" of the world
of objects. Objects certainly cost less to make, so the proportional value of production is shrinking, but they continue to increase in "volume" at the same rate as before.
Objects are just as cumbersome as they ever were. They
still have to be moved around and repaired. No matter
what our vantage point, the great hope of work set free
from the harshness of the physical world of objects has
certainly not been realized, as is witnessed by the continuing increase in the number of wage earners suffering
from physical pain and complaining about having to lift
heavy weights.[4]

But within this tertiarized world, factory workers in
the classic, assembly-line sense have become a minority.
Workers are now maintenance personnel or repairmen
more than factory hands. They function in a setting that
is, for the most part, more a workshop than an assembly line. White-collar employees are likewise a category
undergoing rapid change. In the early 1980s, the majority
of them held administrative jobs in firms or in the public
sector. Today, the majority work in sales or in services

to individuals. The client has become a central figure of their existence—the real order-giver as far as they are concerned, sometimes more so than the boss himself.

The Information Society

This first approach to analyzing the exit from industrial society does not, however, exhaust the question, even in the strict sense of a definition of the careers that are on offer. Researchers studying bacteria or improving the efficiency of microprocessors are also fully within post-industrial society. Jobs like these fall to some extent under the American sociologist Daniel Bell's definition of post-industrial society as a knowledge-based society.[3] Today we are more likely to call it an information society. How should we characterize it?

"The new economy," a term that emerged in the 1990s, sheds some light on the issue. It designates a radical modification of the established paradigm of the economy as analyzed by Adam Smith and Karl Marx. Smith explained that if it takes twice as long to hunt a deer as it does to hunt a beaver, the deer will necessarily cost twice as much, on average, as the beaver. The "new economy" is characterized by a cost structure that is entirely at variance with this schema. It costs a lot to conceive a piece of software, but it does not cost much to manufacture it. In the "new economy," it is the first unit of a manufactured product that is costly; the second unit, and those that follow, bear a low cost, or even, in some limit cases, no cost at all. In Smith's language, we would have to equate all these costs to the time spent killing the first beaver or the first deer—for example, the time spent discovering the animal's lair. In Marx's language, we would have to say that the source of added value is not the labor expended on producing the good but the labor invested in designing it.

Pharmaceuticals are a good example. The hardest part is discovering the right molecule. The actual cost of making the medication (measurable in the price of generic drugs) is much less than the cost of amortizing the outlays on research and development, which are billed to the consumers of branded pharmaceuticals. Many other examples fit the same pattern. In the film industry, it is the shooting and the editing that are costly, not the making of prints. In general terms, information, whether in the form of a digital code, a symbol, or a molecule, costs much more to conceive than the physical support that subsequently contains it.

This paradigm is also relevant to industrial firms. For example, advertising campaigns for Renault, France's symbol of industrial society in the way Ford once was for the United States, try to present the company as a "conceptualizer" of automobiles. And Renault actually does tend to manufacture an ever-declining part of each car that bears its brand. In the 1950s, Renault manufactured 80 percent of each car that was delivered to the dealer. Today it manufactures no more than 20 percent, and Renault's technology and design complex at Guyancourt is the company's largest "industrial" site. It is there that the costly first unit is "manufactured." There is a story (perhaps apocryphal, but nonetheless illustrative) that Volkswagen's head of purchasing in Brazil expressed his satisfaction that the company had succeeded in shifting the core of its manufacturing operation offshore, leaving the head office in Germany to do what it did best: put the VW badge on the automobiles.

This second way of characterizing post-industrial society sheds light from a different angle on the reasons for the dismantling of the industrial firm. In a time of globalization, firms try to re-focus themselves on activities that are planet wide in scope, the ones that reach the greatest number of customers. Immaterial activities, in which the cost is in the first unit (brand promotion, for example), are much more profitable than the fabrication of the goods themselves.

Post-Industrial "Society"

In this way, post-industrial society forges a link between two areas of activity that are, in a sense, at opposite poles: the conception of goods (or even their "conceptualization"—the immaterial domain) and their "prescription" (the many ways, including marketing, by which goods are channeled to the end users for whom they were designed). The chemical formula that encodes a medicine is immaterial. The doctor who puts his ear to the chest of a patient and prescribes the right medicine is in the domain of F2F. In both cases, it is the actual making of the goods that tends to dwindle as a socially pertinent figure.

These developments may seem to make the decline of industrial society natural. Yet on the basis of these same transformations, other outcomes would have been possible—outcomes that might well have reinforced the preceding model instead of destroying it. We can imagine a scenario in which each sector was organized around a few large industrial firms controlling the whole chain of production, upstream in its research laboratories and downstream in its distribution networks, internalizing (as economists say) the activities of conception, manufacturing, and prescription. This was indeed how the "spontaneous" tendencies of the economy were viewed in the 1960s, when John Kenneth Galbraith spoke of "the new industrial state."

Thus, to grasp the nature of post-industrial society, we must review other cases of rupture, and we must also take a closer look at the reasons for the exhaustion of Western industrial society. This will be the theme of my first chapter. We will then have to examine how globalization, the crucial new element on the scene, is helping to reshape the world economies. This will be the topic of my second chapter. Finally, we must try to find out why it seems so difficult today to regulate post-industrial society. This will be the goal of my third chapter, in which I will argue that one of the central paradoxes of our time is that, at the very moment when globalization is opening up borders and posing common challenges to almost all countries, their various social models seem to be drifting apart. Within Europe—economically and institutionally a very homogeneous region—nothing appears more distinct than the British, Scandinavian, German, and French models. If it was natural to speak of industrial society, it is a lot harder to speak meaningfully of post-industrial "society." Never has the awareness that we all live in the same world been so strong. Never have the social conditions of existence been so distinct. Like video games that make it hard for children to live in the real world, post-industrial society widens the gap between the imaginary and the real.[6] The information society accelerates the production of shared vision of the world, and the service society partitions social life into separate segments. In psychoanalytical terms, one could say that the symbolic function, the mediator between the imaginary and the real, has shriveled.

Durkheim envisioned mechanical solidarity among the members of pre-industrial society giving way to organic solidarity among the members of a society governed by the division of social labor. The latter brings into being, according to Durkheim, a system of "rights and duties that bind [humans] among themselves in a lasting fashion."[7] In the world we are entering, one would search in vain for the organic solidarity Durkheim devoutly wished for. The end of the solidarity that was at the core of the industrial world leaves open the question of how we are to conceive of post-industrial "society."

1   The Era of Ruptures

The formidable upheaval in social conditions that has taken place since the early 1980s has been seen by many as a new "great transformation"[1] comparable in scope to the one that occurred in the nineteenth century. Where did this new world come from? Five major ruptures provide keys to the answer.

The first of these ruptures was brought about by what we must call a new industrial revolution. It arrived two centuries after "the" industrial revolution, which began at the end of the eighteenth century and which is associated with the steam engine. Toward the end of the nineteenth century, another revolution took place; its symbol was the harnessing of electric power. From this perspective, we live in the time of a "third industrial revolution."

The next rupture is social. It proceeds from a new way of conceiving human labor. Linked to the new industrial revolution, it nevertheless has its own singular history, which some authors believe would have unfolded in any case.

The third rupture is a cultural revolution, often linked to the flowering of contemporary individualism that was marked in France by the events of May 1968 or in the United States by the Woodstock concert—events that called into question the social norms that had prevailed hitherto.

The fourth rupture originates in the financial markets. After 1929, these markets were subjected to regulatory supervision. Since the 1980s, finance has regained its ascendancy over the business world in general. This too is a singular history, one tied only very indirectly to the others.

The fifth rupture, which will be the topic of my next chapter, is globalization, which we can interpret in narrow and concrete terms as the entry of China and India into the arena of world capitalism. Here again, there is an unprecedented story to tell—a story that owes little to the other ruptures I have outlined.

These ruptures are interarticulated so tightly that they are often confused. Yet each of them flows from a different logic, so let us approach each on its own before attempting to grasp how they interact and combine.

A Technological Revolution

In 1939 Joseph Schumpeter pointed out a few of the features that allow to recognize an industrial revolution. They occur in "clusters" around small numbers of radical innovations, and it is striking that they occur in the seventh decade of each century. In the 1770s, Watt's steam engine, Hargreaves's spinning jenny, and advances in metallurgy (e.g., the first metal bridge was constructed in 1779) led to the onset of industrialization. In the later nineteenth century, it was electricity, the telephone, and the internal-combustion engine that transformed the world. "Our" current industrial revolution emerged in the late 1960s and the 1970s. In 1969, the US Department of Defense developed Arpanet. In 1971, Intel developed the first microprocessor. In 1976, the Apple II, soon to become the model for all desktop computers, went on sale.

In discussing industrial revolutions, economists speak of general-purpose technologies (GPTs).[2] These are technologies with multiple uses whose potential exceeds the intentions and imaginations of their inventors. When electricity was discovered, no one had any idea that it would make possible the invention of televisions or washing machines. Thomas Edison, in a celebrated example, thought that the likeliest use for his gramophone would be to record the oral testaments of the dying. Of course, a GPT fills an initial need. In the case of information technology (IT), the expanding management of information (about customers, about citizens) accounts for the demand addressed to this sector. But a GPT opens up a field of possibilities that goes beyond the initial requirement, propagates through the whole array of industrial sectors, and radically modifies their way of conceiving their own initial needs. The Internet exceeded the intentions of Department of Defense analysts who were looking for a technical answer to an unlikely hypothesis: paralysis of normal military communications in the United States by a nuclear strike. Like electricity a century earlier, the Internet makes it possible to reorganize production. But the extent of this reconfiguration has escaped its creators, who belonged within an earlier logic.

A Social Revolution

This brings us to the second rupture: that in the organization of work. Just as electricity came together with what was to become the "scientific organization of work" (or "Taylorism," after Frederick W. Taylor, 1856–1915), today the IT revolution comes together with a new organization of work that appears to be inseparable from its coming.

The fact that these phenomena are intimately linked does not at all imply that technology automatically produces its own proper mode of social organization. At the moment when electricity was domesticated, nothing allowed contemporaries to think that it would lead to assembly-line production. In fact, they believed at first that it was going to boost small artisans relative to large enterprises—an example that highlights the nature of this indeterminacy. In the nineteenth century, before the age of electricity, factories using steam power relied on a specific organization of work—the "factory system," which operated as follows: A steam engine was placed at the center of the factory to feed energy to the workers. The workers were often paid by the piece, which at the time was the only tangible way to control their efficiency. The boss was the owner, the one who supplied the capital in the form of the steam engine, which replaced natural forms of energy: water, wind, animal, or human power. Nevertheless, from the occupational point of view the internal organization of the factory retained many features of the medieval model of production. There still were craft guilds that replicated the world of "journeymen" and "masters," handing their knowledge down from one generation to the next. The French economic historian Yves Lequin described what it was like to work in a steel mill or a glassworks, emblematic sites of the (first) industrial revolution, as follows: "Empiricism reigned throughout. . . . His eye told the glassmaker or the foundryman to open the furnace because the material inside had melted, the ears of the workman were always attuned to the ambient sounds of the machinery and the surroundings, his nose and his skin told a man that he should draw back from the throat of the blast furnace."[3]

Until the middle of the nineteenth century, the craft worker was the inheritor of the "secrets" of the "corporations." The American Federation of Labor, in an elitist conception of its role, originally restricted union membership to the skilled trades, excluding the unskilled, most of whom were immigrants.

When electricity became available, the small artisans who were losing ground because they could not avail themselves of steam power thought their hour had come. Electricity promised a democratization of access to energy, and it led some to think that soon there would be no more need for "owners" or "capital." This promise anticipated, to some extent, the early days of the information revolution, when a similar assumption was made: that it would put an end to the large industrial organizations of the twentieth century and would promote a new, more artisanal model in which "small" would be "beautiful."

The New Principles of the Organization of Work

The objectives of the organization of work in the Internet age in the rich countries are adaptability to demand, reactivity, quality, and (above all) optimization of the production process, especially through the utilization of the range of human competence. These objectives require more flexible, "multi-skilled" employees, and they allow some delegation of responsibility to lower levels of the hierarchy. It is not hard to see the complementarity between this type of organization of work and the new information and communications technologies. The information society allows producers to offer their customers flexible production, "just-in-time" production, and "made-to-measure" items. The flattening of the hierarchical structure makes it possible to delegate more responsibility to levels that were once closely supervised. Workers, in turn, are more accountable for their performance.

These new methods of production are not a direct offshoot of the IT revolution. They are in part an extension of methods tried out in the 1960s in Japan and associated with the term "Toyotaism." IT does, however, allow a more radical use of these methods, and it creates new applications, out of which came the idea of putting complex production units "online" within and outside the firm. In the 1980s only a few sectors set about reorganizing their modes of production in this way, but as the new methods spread throughout the economy they contributed to the acceleration of productivity in the United States in the 1990s. Three examples will illustrate the organizational paradigm of the contemporary world: that of a typist, that of a salesperson in a large bookstore, and that of a bank teller.

The intrusion of the desktop computer and word processing exposed the typist to formidable competition. Word processing destroyed the typist's work in the simple sense in which printing once destroyed the work of manuscript copyists. Everyone could now "keyboard" his or her own (short) texts: word processing put the art of the typist at everyone's disposal. The principal quality of a typist was the ability to type a text flawlessly the first time through. By making mistakes correctable, word processing made that quality redundant. This example illustrates a point that economists discovered in the 1980s, which is that the new technologies tend to make skilled workers more productive and devalue the work of those less skilled. Managers who used to depend on the labor of typists were now released from this dependency, and their work became more productive. This line of reasoning allows us to see why technical progress was accompanied by rising inequality in the 1980s. There was an oversupply of unskilled labor, so its remuneration had to fall. Skilled work became more productive, so its remuneration could rise.

The second example illustrating the nature of the organizational change is that of a salesperson in a large bookstore, who now performs several tasks at once. He or she manages the inventory in real time, advises customers about what to read, and accompanies them to the checkout counter. The classic vertical hierarchy, in which the execution of a sale obeyed a top-down logic, with each individual performing a specific task in accordance with a plan organized in advance, is replaced by a more flexible organization of work. Where once worker X did as he or she was instructed by foreman Y, who took orders from manager Z, the same person may now receive information, forward it, and take the appropriate action himself. An analogy may be drawn with the system tried in Toyota factories in Japan in the 1960s. The "top-down" system was challenged by a more flexible organization of work that allowed workers to signal to their superiors which individual parts or colors of paint they needed. The goal was to start with the customer and move upstream from there to the production process, and not vice versa as in the heyday of Fordism (when, in the celebrated expression of Henry Ford, customers could choose any color they wanted as long as it was black).[4] Toyotaism was fairly crude in the beginning. To forward their signals, workers noted their requirements on little tickets called *kan ban*. Yet this Toyotaist method marked the beginning of the end of Taylorism, permitting the worker to interrupt the cadence of the production line in order, for example, to reprogram the color of the automobiles coming off it. One of the effects of this kind of reorganization was to reduce the number of managers who had to be employed. This set in motion a process that ultimately would lead to greater inequality. The layers in the middle were occasionally pulled upward, but more often they were sucked down. In the 1950s it was still possible to start out as a worker and, through ability, to win promotion to the ranks of management. Today, one characteristic of being a worker is to remain a worker, deprived of the access to middle management that would make it possible to change one's status. There is now a greater probability of remaining at the bottom of the wage scale for life.

The third example illustrating the organizational changes of the 1980s is the work of a teller in a bank. Thirty years ago, the organization of banks obeyed standard Taylorist logic. You went to one window to get a checkbook, to another window to make a withdrawal, then to a cashier to get your money. No one would have thought of mingling these tasks, any more than one would have thought of assigning the same person to sort the checks and answer the telephone. But today the same employee does almost everything. She cashes checks, gives customers the money they are withdrawing, checks their balances, supplies information about interest-bearing accounts or the use of a credit card, answers the telephone, and presses the button to open the door. If a question addressed to her is too complex, she directs the client to someone more specialized. What is the economic rationale for the emergence of this kind of multi-tasking? None of the rationales already mentioned is very convincing. IT certainly allows certain tasks to be carried out in real time, in a way that was once inconceivable. Thanks to the computer, it is possible to let a customer know on the spot how much money she has in her account. IT also allows the bookseller to manage her stock in real time. But to answer the telephone while one is handing over bills or receiving checks—that rests on principles of organization of work that were entirely conceivable before the IT revolution. This is the thesis of Michael Piore and Charles Sabel,[5] who claim that the new organization of work is not directly linked to new technologies, but rather to new social principles.

What, if not technical progress, is the economic principle that allows us to understand this reorganization of work? The explanation is simple, and once again it comes from Japan. The new organization of work does everything possible to eliminate "idle time." There is no more question, in the world we live in now, of paying someone to do nothing—for example, to wait for a customer to come to one's window. The quest to eliminate idle time (called *muda* or "wastage" in Japanese, and *temps mort* or "dead time" in French) dictates that an employee must always have something to do. The IT revolution is useful here. With the click of a mouse you can resume a task at just the point you had reached when a customer came along to interrupt you. But the principle governing this new organization of work is external to it. It is the automatic consequence of a fundamental datum: the increase in the value of work. Between 1900 and 2000, workers' wages multiplied sevenfold (relative to the price of goods and investments). Hence, any organizational principle that reduces their share of the budget, that in blunt terms permits one person to execute tasks formerly carried out by two, leads to much greater savings (by a factor of 7) than it would have a century ago. In this light we can see the attraction of word processing more clearly: allowing a manager to keyboard his own written communications brings a direct saving in manpower by eliminating the typist. To reduce the work of managing by replacing the foreman with an IT program is "attractive" from the same point of view. Combining the tasks of a cashier and a teller has the same rationale: to reduce idle time. In every case, workers are put under constant pressure to keep them from being idle for any length of time.

This "neo-Stakhanovism" (Philippe Askenazy calls it, in remembrance of the miner who became a hero of Soviet productivity) leads some economists to criticize the idea that the new technologies yield productivity gains in the usual sense of the term, leveraging human work so as to make it more efficient. If there is no more idle time, if people are busy every minute, then they are simply working more, not more productively minute by minute. This evidently goes too far: electronic mail does yield a straightforward gain in productivity over postal mail. But it is an interesting viewpoint nevertheless: the IT revolution is not an "energy" revolution in the way that electricity and the steam engine were. As its name indicates, it is a revolution in information, which in practical terms means a revolution in organization. Thus, there is a close linkage between the IT revolution and the new ways of organizing work, just as there was a linkage between electricity and the end of the factory system, even if it would be wrong in either case to describe the link as one of necessity. A better description would be "opportunistic combination": electricity helped Ford to realize the Taylorist program, and IT allowed Wal-Mart to (in summary terms) realize the Toyotaist program.

Yet, far from signifying the dawn of Jean Fourastié's great hopes for the twentieth century, our post-industrial world is spawning mental and physical disorder. Workplace accidents—far from disappearing, as the tertiarization of the economy seemed to predict—continue to increase.[6] Mental fatigue and stress are becoming commonplace. Modern capitalism emits paradoxical injunctions that workers are not always psychologically well equipped to deal with. ("Give the customer the best possible service, but in the shortest time possible." "Assume responsibilities, but without any effective responsibility for the definition of work.") The iteration of such imperatives is a recipe for heightened anxiety. According to the Organization for Economic Cooperation and Development, the frequency of mental illness among recipients of disability benefit has gone from 17 percent to 28 percent in less than 10 years. But what is sometimes overlooked is the degree to which physical causes of workplace accidents remain significant. Musculoskeletal disorders, for example, have multiplied during the last two decades, becoming the main category among recognized occupational ailments. A particularly illuminating example comes from department managers in retail stores. At one time their job was checking inventory, but that task has been taken over by bar-code scanners. Their mission has changed: it used to consist of checking that no product was missing, and of having missing products replaced. For them, digitization has entailed an increase in physical effort: now they have to bring products to the shelves themselves. Thus, on average, innovations in the organization of work (quality control, rotation of positions, flexible hours of work) are creating an increase in workplace accidents of between 15 percent and 30 percent, the majority of them tied to physical fatigue or to a combination of physical fatigue and mental stress. These pathologies show how optimistic the predictions of Clark and Fourastié were regarding the advent of a service society, which was going to free human labor from physical fatigue. It was not fatigue that marked the bounds of Fordism; it was other forces, economic and social in nature.

The Contradictions of Fordism

From its onset in 1913, Fordism was fraught with an internal contradiction that Henry Ford himself quickly perceived. Scientific Organization of Work (SOW) is, by its very nature, repetitive, boring, "alienating." To get away from it, many workers engaged in absenteeism, forcing the firm to find replacements for them on 24 hours' notice or less. Yet SOW makes the whole line intimately dependent on the willingness of the workers. Henry Ford sought the advice of psychologists and ergonomists but soon realized that none of the remedies they suggested for workers' ennui would do the trick. His stroke of genius was the celebrated decision to double the wages of his workers at one stroke, going to the famous "five-dollar day" where previously the wages had been between $2 and $3 per day. The problems that were keeping the Ford factories from running smoothly evaporated at once. The workers formed a line at the factory doors, and absenteeism was replaced by the desire to perform well. In his memoirs, Ford remarked that he never reduced his cost of production as much as he did the day he doubled his workers' wages.

The legend of Fordism has it that wages were raised in order to allow the workers to buy automobiles—as if Ford, anticipating Keynesianism, created his own market for his own products. This legend is ridiculous on its face. The share of Ford workers in the overall demand for the cars rolling off the assembly line which they themselves manned was infinitesimal. From a balance-sheet perspective, it would have been much simpler to offer workers a free car, keeping wages low so as to reduce the costs passed on to other consumers. Another theory offers a better understanding of the underlying thrust of Fordism: the theory of the efficiency wage.[7] It posits that one can increase the productivity of a worker by raising his wages, whereas the usual notion reverses the sequence: upstream gains in productivity are generally seen as dictating workers' wages downstream. The whole history of Fordism is encapsulated in this paradigm: by raising wages, one increases productivity. Integrating the workers' aspirations into their wages makes it possible to realize them. The bonding of the economic question to the social question within industrial society is illuminated here. The principal goal of the Scientific Organization of Work is to make the less endowed segments of society productive. Engineers and ergonomists strive to make unskilled workers as productive as possible. The burden of the social question, which is to find a way of integrating into society all of its members, is thus assumed by the economy itself. It is not just a matter of giving workers jobs; it is also a matter of seeing that they are productive by organizing production in such a way that they become so. It is this bond between the economic question and the social question that has been broken—a point to which I shall return in the third chapter.

But there was an internal contradiction in Fordism: to buy the willingness of the workers, it was not enough to double their wages relative to what they were earning before; you had to do so relative to what they could earn elsewhere. In itself, earning twice as much as yesterday makes little difference. What really counteracts boredom and stultification is the belief that one is earning more here than one could somewhere else. But the extension of Fordism to the whole economy made this kind of leapfrogging progressively more difficult. Isolated in the midst of a society of traditional craft work, Fordism can thrive. Generalized to the whole of society, it can only wane. The limits of Fordism are reached when wage inflation, having become generalized, no longer leads to productivity gains but now leads to inflation pure and simple—when firms have no other choice but to incorporate every increase in wages into their selling price. The blockage of the system became perceptible in the 1960s and patent in the 1970s (when no more progress in productivity was observed). In the United States it was called "the productivity slowdown."

To this "internal" contradiction of Fordism in the industrialized countries there was added an "external" contradiction that would complete the ruin of the twentieth-century industrial system. It had to do with another notion attributed to Henry Ford: that workers should not be expected to know how to read, or write, or speak English, only to refrain from drinking on the job. Assembly-line work was conceived for an illiterate population, many members of which were recent immigrants to the United States who did not speak English. Taylorism bypassed the old working class, which had progressively constituted itself as a "worker aristocracy" within the confines of the old factory system and which had given rise to the earliest American unions. These unions never dreamed of unionizing the illiterate workers who were arriving from Sicily and Poland—workers they mistrusted but Fordism welcomed. Here was the origin of the "external" contradiction of Fordism. If the first assembly-line workers did not know how to read or speak English, their children and grandchildren certainly did. Educational progress undermined the basis of Fordism.

May 1968

May 1968 was the moment when French students rejected the hierarchical society their parents had endured. The formula "wages equal obedience" was no longer acceptable to them. This protest movement had counterparts in all industrialized countries. University campuses in California experienced the same protest in a different form, focusing on the war in Vietnam. "May '68 was not a purely French event," wrote the 1968 activist (now a French politician) Henri Weber. "Its dimensions, its reality were immediately international. In the United States, in western Europe, in Japan, we are dealing with one and the same movement: the same motivating drives, the same ideologies, the same watchwords, the same practices."[8] The common thread running through these revolts was generational conflict. And the countries in which May 1968 was "severest" were the ones in which the parental generation had the most to answer for: Germany, Italy, and Japan.

The events of May 1968 are often interpreted as an upsurge of individualism at the heart of an industrial

society that remained profoundly holistic.⁹ May 1968
marks an undeniable rupture in the functioning of the
institutions that were exposed to its onslaught: the family,
the factory, schooling. The crisis shifted them from a position in which their legitimacy was innate to one in which
it had to be acquired. In the language of economists, each
of these institutions found itself immersed in a more
competitive environment—an environment in which its
monopoly on authority had been shattered. Each was
deeply affected, undergoing something close to a genetic
mutation so as to adapt to this new environment. Families
rearranged themselves, schooling gave way to pedagogy,
the factory began the process of externalization. Like Ford
putting immigrants who could not read or write to work,
society gradually learned to put its rebellious but now
educated youth to work.

Yet it is misleading to speak breezily about individualism. The young Americans who went to Woodstock
to listen to Jimi Hendrix and the Parisian students who
mounted the barricades didn't look at it that way. The
collective power of their movement was one of the
reasons for its enchanting effect on them. In hindsight,
it is simpler to characterize May 1968 as the emergence
of youth as an autonomous social force. University and
student life implicitly supplied models to the protago-
nists. The link between student life and the aspirations of
youth gives us an important clue for understanding the
technological revolution that took place at the same time.
The technological evolution of the industrial world since

the start of the 1970s will be poorly understood as long as one fails to see that its pioneers were the same Baby Boomers who went on strike in May 1968. It was through IT that students who came of age in the protest culture of the American campuses of the 1960s would find a way to fracture the standardized world created by their parents.[10]

We can assess the "sociology" of these discoveries by tracing the steps that gave rise to the Internet. In 1969, the Advanced Research Projects Agency of the US Department of Defense set up a revolutionary communications network, the purpose of which was to protect military transmissions from the consequences of an atomic strike. The system was increasingly utilized by university researchers under contract to the Department of Defense. It slid into the public domain thanks to modem, invented in 1978 by two students at the University of Chicago who wanted to communicate for free. In 1979, three students (two at Duke University and one at the University of North Carolina) developed a version of the Unix operating system that made it possible to link up computers through a normal telephone line.[11] Thanks to ongoing progress in optical electronics, the technology of digital packet switching took off. The Internet was born from these developments.

The Financial Revolution

The fourth rupture that characterizes our epoch is the financial revolution of the 1980s—in other words, the stock market's seizure of power in the management of companies. After the crash of 1929, the power of the stock exchange lost much of its legitimacy.[12] Shareholders gave up control of companies to managers. In 1932, Adolf Berle and Gardiner Means explained that this delegation of authority was the only possible solution to the contradiction between the growing size of firms and the limited resources of family capitalism.[13] With few exceptions, a single shareholder could no longer hope to own a company of significant size, so shareholders had to agree among themselves to delegate their authority to a manager. The latter was not a shareholder but a salaried employee of the company—one better paid than the others, of course (hence the informal distinction in English between the *wages* of a workman and the *salary* of a manager, where French uses *salaire* for both), but subject to a labor contract that stipulated a set remuneration and rewards in kind for as long as the contract remained in force. J. Pierpont Morgan thought that the top executive of a firm should earn no more than 20 times the average wage of its workers. In the United States today that multiple has risen to 200!

Still, it is not so much the quantitative rupture as the qualitative one that is at stake here. With the financial revolution of the 1980s, managers were hoisted out of the salary-earning class. In the absence of shareholders who were managers, the simple expedient of turning managers into shareholders was adopted. Thanks to stock options, the incentives for heads of firms were brought into line with returns to shareholders, which meant that heads of firms simply ended up behaving like shareholders.[14] The variable portion of the compensation of chief operating officers continues to grow in all countries. It now amounts to more than 60 percent of the compensation of CEOs in the United States, 50 percent in Germany, and 40 percent in France.

In an article suggestively titled "Breach of Trust in Hostile Takeovers," the American economists Andrei Shleifer and Larry Summers highlighted the nature of this divorce between heads of companies and wage and salary earners.[15] They started with an apparently theoretical question: When a corporate raider acquires a company and sells off its assets piecemeal, he generates stock-market gains. How should this increased value be interpreted?

The American economists Richard Ruback and Michael Jensen had shown that target firms increased in value (on the order of 30 percent on average when their study was published, around 15 percent today), and that shareholders in bidding firms did not lose but did not gain either.[16] Overall, Ruback and Jensen had concluded (logically, it would seem) that these gains measured the increase in the productive efficiency of the companies.

Shleifer and Summers offered a different interpretation. From their perspective, every time a raider attacks a company in order to create "value," all he does is expropriate that company's "stakeholders" for the benefit of the shareholders. Let us take an example. Companies normally offer their wage and salary earners the prospect of a career with the firm. The promise of being able to rise through the ranks, or at any rate to earn more with increased seniority, gives the worker an incentive to remain with the company. It is one of the ways, according to the theory of the efficiency wage, of winning the allegiance of the workforce. For the company, though, the higher wages earned by more senior personnel represent an added cost, which is justified only by the pull it exerts on junior personnel. Such "implicit contracts" have a crucial function: to create a "stakeholder" economy. They help a firm to function well, but it is not hard to see why they may also become a hindrance. We could make an analogy with an insurance company that awards a bonus to good drivers and makes bad ones pay a penalty. If the bonuses are too generous, if the population of those benefiting from them grows too large, it may become advantageous to get rid of them. This step may create "value" in the financial sense, but that does not prove that it creates value in the economic sense of increasing the productivity of the entire operation. Stripped of a credible system of reward and penalty, the new company might very well be less efficient than it was before, even though it might be more profitable financially after having repudiated its debt to the good drivers.

When Shleifer and Summers published their article, the productivity gains arising from the IT revolution had not yet become evident. It was the period of Robert Solow's paradox: "You can see the computer age everywhere but in the productivity statistics."[17] By now, though, it is well established that the information age has well and truly generated productivity gains, and that the reorganization undertaken by firms in the 1980s has yielded an improvement in the overall efficiency of the economy. But the analysis of Shleifer and Summers sheds light on a basic rupture: the old equilibrium between markets and organizations has changed. The balance has swung to the side of markets. The organic link binding wage and salary earners to CEOs, to the detriment of sharcholders, in the age when CEOs were salary earners themselves, has broken, and the invisible handshake between management and workers has relaxed.[18]

In the 1980s it was the fashion to reduce the size of firms, to "downsize." Raiders broke up large conglomerates, selling off their subsidiaries piecemeal, refocusing their activities, and transferring tasks considered nonessential to subcontractors. Umbrella makers stopped making bathing suits, and wage earners experienced new wage instability.[19] When this job was done, firms could begin growing again, starting in the 1990s, in the sole area of their "core business." The wave of mergers and acquisitions, still ongoing, bears witness to this. It also proves that size was not the major problem that "downsizing" was trying to solve.

Conclusion

We have come full circle. On all sides, contemporary capitalism is thoroughly dismembering the industrial firm.

The Fordist pyramid is being carved into thinner and thinner slices. Hierarchies are becoming flatter. Firms are focusing on their comparative advantages. Engineering bureaus are now independent entities, and the manufacturing has been outsourced, even relocated abroad. There is no single cause for this rupture. It can be read as an assault on unions. The first companies to be restructured in the United States were the most unionized ones. The new capitalism is breaking the worker collectives that were built up in the course of the last century, and is doing so largely for that very reason, just as the Scientific Organization of Work had flouted the worker aristocracy a century earlier. But external factors also play an important part. The revolt against assembly-line work in May 1968, and the emergence of new technologies, have allowed the coming of a "new spirit of capitalism."[20] There are grounds for seeing this rupture as paradigmatic. Capitalism has begun to rethink the organization of work. Its social intelligence has been mobilized in a direction running counter to Fordism: no longer to make unskilled workers productive, but to make possible factories without workers.

2 The New World Economy

The crisis of industrial society in the rich countries is being paralleled in astonishing fashion by the equally revolutionary change that we are seeing on the world scene. The East-West confrontation, which, as Raymond Aron put it, instantiated two possible facets of industrial society, yielded with brutal suddenness, in the 13 years between the death of Mao and the fall of the Berlin Wall, to opposition between North and South, marked by the arrival at the table of world capitalism of the enormous population blocs of China, India, and the countries of the former Soviet Bloc. How are we to conceptualize the formidable simultaneity between this development and the internal transformation of capitalism? Is it fortuitous, or is there a logic to it?

It is possible, to begin with, to trace the crisis of the "East Bloc" countries to the exhaustion of the dynamism of industrial society, which was grounded in a hierarchical model perfectly adaptable to totalitarian regimes with planned economies. Henry Ford was captivated

by Nazism, and Hitler's sole aim, when it came to productivity, was to import the Fordist model. After 1929,
in fact, there was a tendency to turn the question around
and wonder whether market economies could even
keep up with planned ones. The intellectual success of
Keynesianism in the Western countries depended largely
on the fact that it gave hope to market economies in what
seemed like a losing battle. Raymond Aron's eighteen
lectures on industrial society can likewise be read as an
attempt to restore a balance that seemed to be tilting in
favor of the planned economies.[1]

Yet the question remains: Why, in 1975, did the over-
whelming majority of the poor countries prefer the planning model to the market economy? To answer this in full,
we would have to weigh the national peculiarities of each
country: Russia is not India, and India is not China. But
one causal factor outranks all the others and permits us to
take a unified view of this sequence. What all these countries had in common was that they participated, unsuc-
cessfully in most cases, in the first globalization, the one
that occurred in the nineteenth century. And for all these
countries the lesson was the same: international trade
is unequal in its effects; it favors the prosperity of those
who are already rich, but it does not allow the poorer
countries to catch up with the more advanced ones. This
first globalization would convince them, at the dawn
of their independence, that it was necessary to choose
another path: that of protectionism. A brief review of the
salient facts of the globalization of the nineteenth century

will be helpful here, for it illustrates the potential and the hazards of the globalization that is now commencing.

The First Globalization

The parallels between the nineteenth-century globalization and the current one are striking. The first of these is the similarity of the leading powers. Great Britain dominated the world of yesterday in a manner that perfectly anticipates the American manner today. Trading powers both, they would typically promote free trade wherever they held (and hold) sway. Great Britain was not a colonial power interested only in projecting its political power abroad; it also conceived its might as a way of favoring its economic interests abroad. Clearly that did not prevent it from attempting to control the international balance of power, but in China and in India its first move was to favor English industry by opening up markets to it.

A second and deeper analogy between the globalization of the past and that of today is that each was borne along by a revolution in the technologies of transportation and communications. There is sometimes a tendency to think that the Internet revolution, through which the click of a mouse can link up, if not human beings, then at least their computers, is a distinctive badge of the contemporary world. But the true breakthrough in this domain is to be found in the nineteenth century. At the end of the eighteenth century, it was still common to travel from one town to another on foot, and it took several days for a letter to reach a recipient living 300 kilometers from the capital. With the invention of the telegraph, and the laying of overland and submarine cables, information took less than 24 hours to get to Bombay from London. Along with this revolutionary capacity to exchange information went the development of means of transportation by land and sea, such as the railroad and the steamship, that allowed merchandise and people to follow these flows of information. When the refrigerated ship was developed, in the last quarter of the nineteenth century, frozen beef from Argentina and butter from New Zealand could be imported to Europe.

One indicator of this unprecedented ease in circulating merchandise and information is the differentials in the quoted prices for raw materials in different places. In the middle of the nineteenth century, the differentials in the quoted price of wheat in Chicago, London, and Bombay were still considerable—as much as 50 percent. In 1913, as World War I was about to bring down the curtain on the nineteenth-century globalization, the price differentials were no more than 15 percent, which meant both that individuals knew the prices being quoted elsewhere in real time and that they were able to ship merchandise from where it was cheap to where it was dear.[2]

To extend the comparison, we might note that the present globalization lags behind its predecessor in at least two essential dimensions: financial globalization and international migration. In 1913, the City of London exported 50 percent of English savings abroad. In the case of France, a quarter of the national savings was invested overseas. These are high figures, far higher than those that obtain today. The slow decline of Britain throughout the nineteenth century may be imputed in part to the bias of the City of London in favor of investment overseas rather than at home, which deprived the English economy of the virtuous circle of reinvestment of the profits of past accumulation. No emerging country today can count on inflows of financing comparable to those from which Argentina, Canada, and Australia benefited then.[3]

Another dimension in which the globalization of the past outstripped our own is international migration. Today we live in a world in which the mobility of persons seems very high. But in 1913, 10 percent of the world's population was composed of immigrants, in the straight-forward statistical sense of persons residing in a country different from that in which they were born. The corresponding number today is no more than 3 percent of the world's population. That is obviously an imposing figure in sheer bulk, but relative to the world's population it remains three times smaller than the one a century ago.

Another item illustrates the gap between yesterday's globalization and today's: respect for contracts and private property. Looking at the British Commonwealth alone, it is possible to state that judicial integration back then was also more advanced than today. A contract signed in Bombay was just as enforceable in court as one signed in London. Inasmuch as many economists maintain that the failures of globalization today are due in part

to the judicial risks that beset multinational firms overseas, once again we observe a more fully realized integration in the nineteenth century.[4]

From all these vantage points, whether it be financial
globalization, respect for contracts, population movement, or drastic change introduced by the means of communication, everything indicates that the globalization of
the nineteenth century is not a bit inferior to that of today.
It supplies a test case of globalization in virtually pure
form, offering historians, and above all politicians, the
means to assess its spontaneous effects. The result is stark
and unambiguous. Globalization quite simply proved
incapable of diffusing the prosperity of the richest to the
poorest. Indeed, what we witness during the nineteenth
century is a formidable increase in inequality worldwide.
To confine ourselves to the most representative example
of this trend, England in 1820 was (already) twice as
wealthy per capita as India.[5] But in 1913, at the close of
the first globalization, the income gap had gone from 1:2
to 1:10. What we have here is a fivefold increase in the
wealth gap between rich and poor. On the other hand,
over the same period a process of convergence occurred
between England and the other major European nations,
headed by France and Germany, even though they chose
to follow the path of protectionism.

All the countries that would later become the "Third
World" drew a simple lesson from this long episode:
world trade is not a source of enrichment for poor nations.
When their independence allowed them to set trade poli-

cies for themselves, protectionism was the option these countries preferred. After 1945, the role of the "Third World" in global trade continued to shrink, its exports going from 28 percent of international trade in 1955 to 14 percent in 1972, while its share of the world's population continued to grow. The lesson the twentieth century taught the Third World countries, however, was no more encouraging. By choosing the path of protectionism and cutting itself off from the resources that global capitalism can offer, a poor country does not put itself in a better position to catch up with the rich countries. It loses access to inventions devised in the rich countries, is forced to reinvent the wheel, and ultimately adds new handicaps to the ones it already had to face. The gap in wealth per capita between rich and poor countries shrunk no more during the twentieth century than it had during the nineteenth.[6] So the consensus in favor of protectionism began to crumble. Starting in the 1980s, and at an accelerating pace in the 1990s, the poor countries returned, in their different ways, to the path of global trade. Beginning in 2001, the increase in trade was greater along the North-South axis than along the North North axis. A new international division of labor is arising, with the emerging countries full participants.

Back to the (International) Division of Labor

For the purpose of understanding the forces that are shaping the international division of labor today, and comparing them to those of the nineteenth century, it will be helpful at this point to revisit the theoretical foundations of the latter. The obligatory starting point in this domain is the theory proposed at the start of the nineteenth century by the English economist David Ricardo. Ricardo's theory adopts the intellectual framework developed by Adam Smith in *The Wealth of Nations*. The market impels everyone—the individual in Smith, the nation in Ricardo—to specialize in a single task: the one at which he, or it, excels relative to others. It is not a matter of choosing the task at which one is better than others in absolute terms (a principle that would leave a great many people forlorn); it is a matter of choosing the task at which one is better relative to the other things one might also be capable of doing. For Smith, one chooses to be a baker or a shoemaker on the basis of a simple calculation: knowing one's own skills, one's own cognitive and financial endowment, and what occupation will give one the highest "return" (not necessarily in strictly financial terms only, but from the more general outlook of the pleasures and hardships it entails).

An important property of a market economy, as Adam Smith understood it, is to allow everyone to make this assessment without having to wonder whether, if one chooses to become a shoemaker rather than a baker, one risks not having any bread to eat. In a market economy, in Smith's most celebrated formula, one can count on bread's being available, not because of the baker's benevolence (which would give his customers little assurance), but because of the baker's self-interest. Smith's great contribution to modernity was to have conceived the possibility of a life in society in which the dependence of each person on everyone else was governed by the anonymous forces of the market (an institution that had always existed, of course, but which no one had hitherto imagined playing the cardinal role that it has since come to play).

For Ricardo, the reasoning that was true for individuals was also true for nations. On the basis of this simple parallel, Ricardo pleaded in favor of free trade. International commerce allows each nation to specialize in the activity or the sector in which it enjoys a comparative advantage relative to others. It generates wealth for the nation, as it does for the individual. Does this theory help us to understand the formidable rise in inequality we observe during the nineteenth century? Actually, the theory of international trade predicts nothing with respect to inequality. It merely indicates that one will always gain by trading with others; it does not exclude that the other party will gain more from the trade than oneself. Let us return to the analogy with individual choice, however. It is entirely possible that a person hesitating between two occupations may choose the wrong one, deciding to be a shoemaker just when people have made up their minds to go barefoot or when new machinery is being introduced that can make all the shoes that are needed by itself. If, for these or other reasons, the price of shoes collapses, shoemakers will regret their choice. Clearly, though, the next generation will react, making the shoemaker's trade a rare one and raising its value. Smith's demonstration of the "gravitation" of prices to a natural level is intended to explain this process. It is difficult to understand, in terms of this reasoning, how there can be a long-term slide into poverty. But, as was noted above, inequality between Britain and India multiplied by a factor of 5 during the nineteenth century, though they were bound by a free-trade agreement. How to account for this? Let us attempt to go beyond Ricardo's theory, and pose the problem of individual choice once more, adducing an up-to-date example: I am hesitating between becoming a mathematician and becoming a tennis player. What happens in the case, statistically improbable but theoretically crucial, in which I am completely indifferent between these two options? Two strategies are conceivable. One consists of tossing a coin and letting chance decide my preference, avoiding the fate of Buridan's ass, dying for being unable to make a choice. The other consists of saying to myself "I could do both: mathematics in the morning and tennis in the afternoon, spicing up the monotony of a single occupation with some variety to boot." *A priori*, and from a strictly Ricardian point of view, nothing makes either strategy preferable. Common sense, however, immediately tells me that the second solution, pursuing both careers at once, is the wrong one. To be a good tennis player, one must spend a lot of time training, hitting balls morning and afternoon. To be a good mathematician, one must likewise devote oneself to full-time study. To want to be both is to expose oneself to the risk of being a mediocre mathematician and a bad tennis player—of being outranked by others who chose to specialize. Virtually every economic activity contains an element that economists call "returns to scale": the more I produce, the more productive I become. If I have to make a large investment in order to become competent, it is better to amortize this investment over the largest possible market, or the longest possible time span. This why the first strategy, the coin toss, is the right one. It is preferable to bet everything on either one or the other of the two occupations between which I am torn. Specialization is necessary, even in cases in which Ricardian theory would render it pointless *a priori.*

If this is the basis of the division of labor in the sense understood by Adam Smith, then, applied to international or interregional trade, the implications are very different from those suggested by Ricardian theory in its most elementary form. Let us consider two initially isolated regions. One is rich on account of large initial investments: its infrastructure is denser, its workers are better educated. The other is poor because it lacks these things. What dynamic will play out if trade between these two regions suddenly becomes possible?[7] The richer region will be able to get richer because it will gain access to a new market, thus benefiting from greater economies of scale. But what about the poor region? Whereas the rich region disposes of a wide range of products and talents, the poor region can only specialize in a limited number of activities. A polarization sets in and, to adopt a typology from the French historian Fernand Braudel, it rigidifies into an opposition between a prosperous center and a poor periphery. The center is rich, not because it is specialized, but because it fosters specialization on the part of each of its members. It is itself a setting in which numerous activities can cohabit—in which you can find doctors, hairdressers, auto mechanics, and IT experts. The periphery, in contrast, can only specialize in a handful of tasks: it will make porcelain or textiles, activities in which, through extreme specialization, it can outdo the metropolitan center. But the cost of that will be a loss of diversity, and ultimately greater vulnerability, for if another poor region were to choose the same area of specialization, it might crowd the first one out.

The schema that emerges is nothing like the one imagined by Ricardo, in which each region specializes for the greater benefit of all. Instead it is a scheme of asymmetry between the poor regions, ultra-specialized and vulnerable to competition from other peripheries, and centers that are multi-faceted and thus better hedged against the ups and downs of trade. Such a dynamic is exactly what we observe in the nineteenth century, when the railroads brutally reduced the costs of communication between the regions of France. France was then "as full as an egg," in the words of the French historian Emmanuel Le Roy Ladurie. An agricultural country, it exploited every piece of cultivatable land, over the whole of its territory. The railroad created great hopes on the part of the most outlying regions, like the great expectations created among small artisans by electricity. They counted on the rail-roads' bringing them closer to the large cities, giving them access to markets in which they could sell more and buy more. The problem with trains, as economists would later put it, is that they run both ways. Products from the large cities flowed out to villages and hamlets, destabilizing the outlying regions and provoking an exodus of their workers. In the language of theorists of economic geography, the "forces of agglomeration" prevailed over the "forces of dispersion." A cumulative effect may be triggered. If workers have a choice, they will quit the poor region and go where they can earn higher pay. The poor region wanes while the rich region waxes; people choose to work and invest in the rich region because its infrastructure allows them to be more productive.

The New World Economy

Let us now try to see how the ideas presented above help us to understand the new international division of labor. The well-known Barbie doll supplies an excellent illustration of the nature of world trade today. Barbie's raw materials, the plastic and the "hair," come from Taiwan and Japan. Assembly was done in the Philippines, before it was moved to Indonesia and China, where wages were lower. The molds come from the United States, and the last touch of paint is applied there before the dolls go into the stores. What we have here is not sectoral specialization (textiles for some, automobiles for others). Specialization

applies here to the tasks accomplished by each in order
to fabricate a given product. This "vertical disintegration
of production" is simply the worldwide reflection of the
dismantling of Fordist production analyzed in the previous chapter.[8]

Thus, if we want to comprehend the extent of the
rupture that came about in the 1990s, it will be much more
helpful to analyze how the chain of value of a good tends
to deform than to concentrate on rivalry between sectors.
A pair of Nike shoes supplies another striking example
of the processes at work. Consider the Air Pegasus
model, which costs $70 in the United States. The wage
of the (probably female) worker who makes the shoes is
$2.75 per hour. How can one earn so little for making a
product that sells for so much? The answer emerges from
a full tally of the costs incurred. To start with, the cost of
manufacturing is greater than just the cost of the labor.
Leather, textiles, and machinery are needed to assemble
the shoes, to which are added the costs of transportation
and customs. All these factors together yield a total of
$16, which is what it costs Nike to take delivery of the
shoes at the port of Los Angeles. To this material cost is
then added all the outlays Nike will have to make so as to
transform this physical object into a social object—that is,
into a basketball shoe that people will want to buy. This is
the core of what the Nike company does: it makes these
basketball shoes recognizable and desirable by spending
money on advertising and promotions that show them on
the feet of great athletes, which cause television viewers

throughout the world to want to wear them too. The sum of these outlays is equal to the cost already borne in fabricating the physical object itself, so the total cost of the shoes has doubled to around $35 for manufacture and promotion combined. Half of the selling price of the shoes is now accounted for: it costs as much to make the physical object and ship it to the United States as it does to make it desirable as a social object. So how do we get from $35 to the $70 charged to the retail customer? The answer is simple: still to pay are all the costs necessary to put it physically on the customer's foot—in other words, all the expense of distribution.

This cost structure perfectly illustrates, in schematic fashion, the contours of post-industrial society as it was delineated in the introduction. Conceptualization and design upstream, and "prescription" downstream (in the sense given this word in the introduction: all the myriad ways of getting a pair of these shoes onto the feet of the end user) become the core activities of rich countries. The middle stage, fabrication, becomes non-essential and can be externalized.[9] In the new international division of labor, the rich tend to sell immaterial goods and buy material goods. The prescription of goods, the F2F, is by definition not subject to international exchange.

In the language of the new theories of international trade, the rich countries specialize in the segment of production in which the returns to scale are greatest. In the case of Nike, all it takes is for the star team to be wearing that pair of basketball shoes on the night of a world championship final for the whole planet to want to wear them too. A given outlay, the sponsoring of eleven players, instantaneously produces a worldwide payoff. Similarly, the discovery of a new vaccine represents a fixed cost (the expense of research and development) that can then profit the entire world, without further expenditure. The greater the number of beneficiaries, the easier it will be to amortize the costs of research, and the more profitable it will be to undertake further research. The difference from the industrial era plays out here. In the industrial era, the bulk of the expense was incurred not so much in convincing consumers to buy a car as in making it at the lowest possible cost.

One of the major challenges for the emerging countries is how to gain their share of immaterial production by becoming producers of concepts and of designs. There is no guarantee that they will achieve this. Mexico has earned its stripes as a subcontractor for the United States but has not succeeded in becoming a center to rival the United States. The bulk of employment in Mexico was once around Mexico City, but it has gradually migrated to locations along the border, to assembly facilities (*maquiladoras*) that are highly dependent on North American prime manufacturers. Mexico is experiencing globalization as a periphery in competition with other peripheries, under the constant threat that prime manufacturers may change their strategies.

China, in contrast, is creating new metropolises on its Pacific coast, intended to endow it with all the attributes of power. The Chinese model conforms to that of Japan, which proved that a country could profit from globalization as long as it organized its own "primitive accumulation" of the factors of growth. As was true of Japan before it, the rate of savings in China is today very high—close to 50 percent. The schooling of children is equally remarkable: less than 20 percent of the Chinese population is illiterate. The lesson of the nineteenth century was heeded: The international division of labor does not produce prosperity. It only helps those who help themselves first. For poorly endowed countries, where infrastructure is sparse and the population is poorly educated and exposed to public health problems, the multinational corporations are not much help; they simply go elsewhere.

The Globalization of Images of Globalization

If globalization does not automatically spread material prosperity to all poor countries, it certainly does broadcast images of it. In this sense, the current globalization is fundamentally different from the ones that went before: anyone can now become a spectator of a world in which, very often, one cannot participate as an actor. In the world Braudel described in terms of center and periphery, the further a traveler moved away from the center, whether it was Venice, Genoa, Antwerp, Amsterdam, or London, the farther back he receded in time. Prosperity declined, and so did the intensity of life. Far from the city, people lived as they had in the past, sometimes in the remote past, as

though history had flowed by more slowly. The intensity
of "modern life" was missing there, because in essence it
was unknown. Today it is much harder to experience that
kind of distancing effect. The diffusion of images originating at the center is universal; there is not a remote village
anywhere—provided it has electricity—that they do not
reach. This is an utterly novel aspect of modernity. The
poor half of the world, the half that lives on less than $2
per day, is without the attributes of the rich world. But its
aspirations are indexed to it.

Not everything about this gap between expectation and
reality is negative, as we see if we focus on the essential
question of demography. Female fertility does in fact
show how the globalization of images transforms behav-
ior, even when material conditions remain unchanged.
The demographic explosion in developing countries
is both very well known, and very controversial. A few
numbers will give the measure of the phenomenon.
Egypt, an Islamic country, has gone from 13 million
inhabitants in 1913 to 70 million today, and should reach
100 million in 2025. Brazil, very Catholic, went from 50
million in 1950 to 150 million inhabitants today. Between
the beginning and the end of the twentieth century, India
went from 300 million inhabitants to more than a billion
(that is, a thousand million).

Demographic transition is the term used for the process
of moving from a regime of high fertility to one of low
fertility. High fertility is, let's say, more than 6 children
per woman; low fertility is less than 2.1 children per

woman (the threshold that guarantees demographic sta-
bility). This transition is happening now, at an extremely
rapid rate, and the phenomenon does not stop at civiliza-
tional boundaries. Take Egypt once again: in 1950 census
data showed 7 children per woman; today the figure is
3.4. At that pace, there is no doubt that the demographic
transition will be complete by 2025. Or take another
Muslim country: Indonesia, the most populous. In 1950
the average there was 5.5 children per woman, today it
is 2.6, and the end of the demographic transition is near.
The trend in India is comparable: the country went from
6 to 3.3 children per woman over the same period.

   According to United Nations forecasts for the planet as
a whole, the demographic transition will be achieved by
2050, and starting from that date the world's population
will commence a decline (which may be inexorable). We
are "losing" one child per woman per decade on average,
and nothing ensures that female fertility will stabilize
at 2.1 children per woman. If couples prefer 2 children
on average, the figure that currently obtains in the rich
countries, it is quite possible that the point of equilibrium
may be strictly inferior to this level, given the simple fact
that not all women marry. We are not there yet, but the
speed at which we are getting there is startling. There is
one major exception to this general rule: Africa. In that
continent, the world's poorest, female fertility remains
very high: today it is calculated to be still 6 children per
woman. Yet there are hints that the transition is commencing even in Africa. According the United Nations, African

women could be heading towards 3.5 children in 2025, as opposed to 5 now, and 7 in the mid 1970s. Pakistan is another counterexample, which the thicket of transformations taking place in the other Muslim countries sometimes hides from view.

Returning to the planet-wide situation, we may ask why this demographic transition is occurring. An explanation often given by economists is that the tipping point comes when the opportunity cost of raising children increases. What that means in the vernacular is "when women have better things to do." When women are offered employment and a wage, the social demand for children diminishes. According to the American economist Gary Becker, a virtuous circle may then start up.[10] People have fewer children, but they take better care of them. Parents try to ensure a better future for them through schooling. The paradox of the current demographic transition lies in the fact that it is occurring even though material conditions have not really (yet) changed in many of the countries where it is taking place.[11] It is observed in the rural world and in the cities, whether women are working or not, and sometimes even before the impact of schooling has made itself felt.

The explanation given by the United Nations is that the women of the world see on television a way of life that fascinates them: that of Western women. Through the images to which they have access, they enter a world very remote in material terms from the one they are living in yet sufficiently near to generate a desire to behave as though they had already entered it. Brazilian television has proved to be much more potent than the Catholic Church, even though the Church has been able to block family planning. Demography is perhaps the most important factor in human history. What we see here is an illustration of the impact on demography of this gap between virtual globalization and real globalization. It constitutes one of the major questions of the contemporary world, for the rich countries as much as for the poor ones: how to reconcile life as it is lived with the life that is aspired to when modes of social mediation are becoming scarce.

What Is at Stake in the World to Come

The fact that the planetary demographic transition will be complete by 2050 does nothing to lessen the challenges that are going to continue to mount between now and then. Over that short span of time, the world's population is going to grow by more than 50 percent, essentially through a swelling of the poor population. Today the world holds 6 billion human inhabitants: 1 billion rich ones, 1 billion who aspire to become rich, and 3 billion poor ones, in the mathematical sense that they earn less than $2 per day. By 2050 the world's population will peak at 9 billion inhabitants (and begin to decline). Of those, perhaps 2 billion will be rich, 2 to 3 billion will be aspirants, and 4 to 5 billion will be very poor. What this means is that the world of 2050 will see the present difficulties multiplied: there will be twice as many rich people, which

will pose considerable ecological problems. And the mass
of poor people will still be there, more numerous than
today, which means that the imbalance between wealth
and poverty will still be huge.

The world will have to face difficult and urgent problems caused by these disequilibria. The ecological
problem is, past all doubt, the most important. The planet
cannot sustain an extension of current Western modes of
ecological consumption to China and India. Where can
we look for consensus in this area? The world is moving
toward a multipolar structure. Besides the United States,
Europe, and Japan, there are already two new candidates
for regional hegemony, China and India, and they will
be joined by other power centers (in Africa, the Middle
East, and Latin America) that will want to play a role;
nor has Russia gone away. The American political scientist Samuel Huntington is right about this much: the West
is not going to hold onto its monopoly of prosperity for
long. The near future might resemble nineteenth-century
Europe, where competition between France and Germany
to outstrip Britain laid the ground for the cataclysm of the
twentieth century. Only by creating a multilateral order
endowed with legitimate institutions capable of defusing
the conflicts that the spontaneous evolution of the world
is preparing will it be possible to avoid the risks of a multipolar and unstable world.[12]

A race against time is under way. Either a "just" multilateral system will succeed in imposing itself and gaining
sufficient legitimacy to pacify relations between the blocs

of the future or the multipolar reality will remain fragile and contested and the rise of foreseeable tensions (over access to raw materials, for example) will become dangerous. Europeans (who know better than anyone else, from experience, what tragedies rivalry between nations can lead to) have a message to communicate to the world about this. Will they communicate it?

Conclusion

Globalization is the fifth of the ruptures that make it possible to understand the emergence of post-industrial society. Rather than burdening ourselves with the rather empty question of whether it is the cause or the effect of the other ruptures, it will be more useful to consider it as a dimension of post-industrial society, the main tendencies of which it highlights with great clarity. The "vertical disintegration" of the production line at the international level, to start with, is a reflection of the process of externalization of work begun within the industrial countries. Like the Internet, production follows a great variety of routes to arrive at its goals. The largest industrial companies become much more the strategists than the hands-on operators of a skein of production distributed around the world.

The international division of labor also illuminates why the organic solidarity on which Durkheim counted is hard to find. The market does not create a tightly knit community of outcomes and interests. The new theories of international trade, based on the quest for returns to scale, tell us why: the market stimulates a race to accumulate strategic factors, which makes trading partners into rivals much more than sharers in solidarity. Recent work by Philippe Martin, Thierry Mayer, and Matthias Thoenig shows that trade in general does not promote peace in international relations. Montesquieu's beautiful thoughts on "le doux commerce des hommes" ("sweet trade among mankind") are going to have to be revised.[13]

Finally, globalization illuminates one of the most important aspects of post-industrial society: the growing disparity between a global information society and the territorial reality of a divide between wealth and poverty. Demography gives a positive example of this disparity. The events of September 11, 2001, organized as a TV show, illustrate its macabre side.[14]

3   Is There a European Social Model?

For as long as the world was divided into two blocs, East and West, the construction of what has become the European Union appeared to be the best way of bringing Europeans together and keeping their internal conflicts from offering any purchase to the "Communist enemy." It was a time when, to paraphrase Guy Debord, Europe could define itself by what it did not wish to be.[1] With the fall of the Berlin Wall, two related phenomena occurred. First, the breakup of the Soviet Union meant that the "communist menace" no longer loomed on the horizon. That opened the way for Europe to expand and take in the countries of the former Eastern Bloc. With that, a new conception of Europe arose: the idea of Europe as a protective "fortress" was replaced by the idea, which had not been foreseen, of Europe as a gate to the world economy. Second, the fall of the Berlin Wall called "the European model" into question. Europe, which had invented social security (in its two variants, Beveridgean and Bismarckian), is struggling today to define a new social model to bear this name. Far from convergence, what we have been witnessing instead for the last 20 years is increasing differentiation between social models within the European Union. While globalization does stimulate a certain convergence of behaviors (as we saw with regard to demography in chapter 2), it also reawakens a number of national singularities that had been thought buried for good. When faced with an uncertain and fearful environment, countries tend to rely on their cultural idiosyncrasies.

Three European Models

To speak of a single European social model covering the United Kingdom, Sweden, Italy, and France makes virtually no sense. Various typologies are possible, allowing us to form an idea of the historical origins of this diversity. From a philosophical point of view, a study by the French sociologist Philippe d'Iribarne titled "Three Figures of Liberty" is particularly fascinating.[2] D'Iribarne analyzes three distinct ways of conceiving liberty in England, Germany, and France as they were shaped in the Middle Ages. These three conceptions illuminate the different ways of thinking about social solidarity today.

The first figure of liberty studied by d'Iribarne is the English one. For an Englishman, to be free means not to belong juridically to anyone else, to be neither the slave nor the serf of another, to be the proprietor of oneself. This figure of liberty was expounded with utmost clarity by John Locke. I am free if the product of my labor belongs to me. At the core of this notion of liberty is the labor market. This explains why countries with a British heritage display a visceral attachment to full employment. This includes the United States, where, according to Joseph Stiglitz, the primary goal of social policy is full employment.

The second figure of liberty is German. In the Kantian formulation, the free man is the man who is not a slave to his passions, and who is able to submit to the categorical imperative of life in society. For a German, to be free is to be recognized as such by others. It means having the right to take part in deliberations, to be seated around the same table as the other free men and be listened to. Jürgen Habermas's theory of "communicative action" reprises this conception.

The third figure is the one originating in France, where the free man is the man who is not in a state of feudal subservience to a superior. His liberty is political. The Frenchman likes to compare himself to the citizens of the ancient city-states. The significance of this liberty is juridical (I have the same political rights as the next man), but also psychological (I am free if I can look an aristocrat in the face with no fear of his contempt). D'Iribarne speaks of a "logic of honor" which a worker may adopt relative to his boss when he is on strike. This conception is reprised, for example, in the opposition between "dominators and dominated" proposed by the French sociologist Pierre Bourdieu. The French definition of liberty is more complex and contradictory than the others. The French model is neither individualist in the English manner nor communitarian in the German manner. There inheres in it (still according to d'Iribarne) a contradiction between two value systems which France has never been able to reconcile: the clerical and the aristocratic. The vector of the former was the Catholic Church, which glorified the equality of all before God. The aristocracy, in contrast, valued *noblesse* (the gentlemanly way) of conduct and sentiment as the badge of its distinction from common folk. Incapable of reconciling these two value systems, France is condemned to sink into hypocrisy at best, and into ignorance of itself at worst. "Already in pre-revolutionary France," d'Iribarne writes, "to treat another person as one's equal in church did not entail doing the same in daily life." The Revolution prolonged this ambivalence, abolishing noble privileges and then immediately creating the "Grandes Écoles," separate from the universities and highly selective, which are meant to supply the nation with its own Republican aristocracy.

The dichotomy between the Grandes Écoles and the French universities is in itself a good illustration of this French duality. The university is the heir of clerical values: admission is non-selective, whereas the high status of the Grandes Écoles is grounded in exclusivity. The French model of Grandes Écoles, seen in the most positive light, abolishes the social origin of its elites. Those who gain admission to the École Normale Supérieure or the École Polytechnique instantly cease to be the sons of workers or daughters of farmers, acquiring the same rank as their classmates; the greatness of this meritocratic model is undeniable. But today it has been corrupted by the social endogamy which it provokes by virtue of its own Malthusianism. Terrorized by the thought that their children might not make it into a Grande École, the upper classes engage in pre-emptive and ever more precocious educational warfare, sometimes as early as kindergarten. The République Française ceases to be one and indivisible and becomes a battleground of social reproduction.

The Three Worlds of the Welfare State

Philippe d'Iribarne's threefold typology bears comparison with the ideas of the Danish sociologist Gosta Esping-Andersen, author of the important book *The Three Worlds of Welfare Capitalism* (Polity, 1990). Esping-Andersen distinguishes liberal, corporatist, and social-democratic versions of the welfare state. The essential point of his theory is to show that the large-scale tendencies of industrial societies, whether in urbanization, growth, or schooling, are far from leading to a standard model of the welfare state. National peculiarities and historical compromises specific to each country count for much more. In social-democratic Sweden, a "red-green" class alliance between workers and peasants at the start of the twentieth-century accounts for the universalism of the welfare state, which aims to integrate the whole of society. The Scandinavian countries are in fact the worthy heirs of

German philosophy, concerned as it was with solidarity
between the individual and society.

In corporatist countries, of which Germany and France
are examples, the welfare state arises out of a deliber-
ate attempt to divide the workers' movement. The neo-
corporatist compromise maintains social stratification,
with the workers obtaining advantages in proportion to
the power relations which they construct, sector by sector
and age cohort by age cohort.

The liberal model of the welfare state, finally, directs its
aid to those worst off; this is the outcome of a debate that
goes back to the early nineteenth century—a debate on
the proper scope of charity toward the poor. It connects
with British philosophy, inasmuch as it only helps those
who are having difficulty on their own in asserting their
freedom as independent workers. Through this approach,
the welfare state obliges the middle classes to find their
own insurance against risks covered in other countries by
social security (health, retirement, and so on). The result
is a permanent class barrier between the poor and the rest
of society.

The now classic contrast between Anglo-American
capitalism and the Scandinavian model is the first inter-
pretive grid to emerge from this typology.[3] The former
relies on the proper functioning of markets, the second
on social solidarity. In countries lying between these
extremes, like France, social compromises lead neither
to the pressure for full employment that flows from the
liberal conception nor to the Scandinavian pressure for
solidarity. Continental capitalism is neo-corporatist in

Esping-Andersen's sense. It aims to protect populations that have already established their status. Compensation for being laid off (unemployment insurance benefits, for example) is proportional to the rights that seniority confers on workers.

A Fourth Type of Capitalism

The French economist Bruno Amable has enriched the typology of Esping-Andersen by distinguishing a fourth type of capitalism proper to Europe: Mediterranean capitalism.[4] It is, in principle, the most traditional of all, grounding social solidarity in the family. (In the preface to the revised edition of his work, Esping-Andersen also emphasizes the role played by families.) The implicit goal of the Mediterranean system of production is to preserve the job and the income of the head of the family. It is characterized by a high rate of unemployment among young people and women. To a degree, France espouses German corporatism, with the difference that it does not create a means of integrating young people, as Germany does through apprenticeships. In this respect, France remains a Mediterranean country, inasmuch as it implicitly assumes that the head of the family will step in to take care of wife and children without a job.

Varieties of European Unemployment

The conceptual differences regarding liberty and solidarity are evident in the different ways the European

Table 3.1
Multi-year averages of rates of unemployment, in percent. Rates of unemployment standardized from 1986. For Germany, the data refer to West Germany until 1991. For 2006, the figures marked with an asterisk refer to February 2007, national source compiled by *The Economist*. Sources: OECD online database (http://stats.oecd.org/wbos); Bean 1994 for non-OECD data (italicized).

	1966–1973	1974–1979	1980–1985	1986–1992	1993–1998	1999–2005	2006
Belgium	*2.7*	*6.0*	11.6	8.0	9.4	7.8	8.2
Denmark	*1.0*	*6.0*	8.8	6.6	6.7	4.9	3.8
France	2.0	4.3	8.1	9.3	11.3	9.3	9.1
Germany	0.8	3.4	6.0	5.9	8.4	8.4	8.4
Netherlands	1.9	3.8	10.4	6.6	5.7	3.4	3.9
Italy	3.4	5.3	8.9	9.2	10.9	9.0	6.8*
UK	*3.4*	*5.0*	11.5	8.9	8.1	5.1	5.5*
US	4.5	6.8	8.1	6.3	5.6	5.0	4.6
Japan	1.2	1.9	2.4	2.4	3.2	4.9	4.1
Austria	*1.4*	*1.7*	*3.2*	*3.4*	4.2	4.2	4.8
Finland	2.6	4.6	5.1	5.8	14.5	9.2	7.8
Norway	1.5	1.8	2.6	4.4	5.0	4.0	3.5
Sweden	2.1	2.0	3.2	2.7	9.2	5.7	4.8*
Switzerland	*0.0*	*1.2*	*1.9*	2.4	3.8	3.5	3.2*

countries reacted to the crisis of the 1970s and the rise of unemployment. The speed with which Sweden and Finland returned to low levels of unemployment, notwithstanding the crisis that affected them at the start of the 1990s, or the successful example of Danish flexisecurity, in contrast to France's continuing experience of high levels of unemployment, make palpable the difference between these cases. As table 3.1 shows, unemployment has followed a constellation of trajectories in the course of recent decades, making it difficult to speak of a single European unemployment.

The first thing to note in table 3.1 is the following well-known result: the countries where unemployment was lowest at the end of the 1960s are the ones where it is highest today. This is notably the case in the three large countries of continental Europe—Germany, France, and Italy—since the millennium. This initial observation shows that the question of unemployment cannot be reduced to the analysis of a fixed correspondence over time between, let's say, institutions and a rate of unemployment. As Olivier Blanchard and Justin Wolfers point out,[5] it is the interaction between external shocks and institutions that creates unemployment. In the high-growth Europe of the 1960s, unemployment was much lower than in the United States, and institutions were perfectly adapted to this regime of growth. It is the lack of change of labor market institutions to a new economic environment that is a problem.

The second thing to note is that it was only after 1993 that the gap really opened up between France, Germany, and Italy and the rest of Europe. Since then the majority of European countries have had unemployment rates of about 5 percent. "European unemployment" no longer has any meaning. The pathology is confined to the three major countries of continental Europe.

A simple way of grasping the factors that help to explain the differences in unemployment rates is to compare the rates of entry into (s) and exit from (h) unemployment. The sum of these two rates ($s + h$) is called *turnover*. The long-term unemployment rate of a country is calculated as the ratio between the percentage of workers who lose their jobs (s) and turnover ($s + h$). Table 3.2 presents the results obtained for a subset of countries, which can be compared to the United States.

Table 3.2 brings out a well-known difference between the United States and Europe: the probability of enduring a spell of unemployment, and the probability of returning to employment (turnover), is much higher in the United States. Even in the United Kingdom, the other putative bastion of Anglo-American capitalism, the rates of entry into and exit from unemployment are two times lower than in the United States. Comparison between Denmark and the Netherlands is likewise very telling.

Table 3.2
Unemployment: separations and hirings (2004). Separations and hirings: annual flows of entries into and departures from unemployment with respect to the original populations (total employment/ unemployment). Source: http://stats.oecd.org/wbos/

	Separations (s)	Hirings (h)	Ratio $s/(s + h)$
US	2.02	33.0	5.8%
France	0.45	4.10	9.8%
Denmark	1.01	19.2	5.0%
UK	0.86	17.2	4.7%
Netherlands	0.32	4.60	6.4%

Denmark is the European country where the likelihood of a spell of unemployment is the highest (ahead of the United Kingdom). The Netherlands, on the other hand, is the country where the likelihood of entering unemployment is the lowest, below the French level. The Dutch and Danish rates of unemployment are, however, not very far apart. In the final reckoning, the two countries arrive at results comparable to the United States (for the ratio of both). These examples lead us back to a familiar result: there is no reliable linkage between the turnover and unemployment.[6]

The first conclusion to be drawn is that there is no single path to full employment. This is the main conclusion reached by the revised strategy for employment published by the Organization for Economic Cooperation and Development in 2006; it emphasizes that there exist several institutional combinations through which unemployment can be reduced. Despite whatever formal similarities may exist between the United Kingdom and Denmark, when it comes to entry into and exit from unemployment, the institutional framework is totally different. Denmark pays high unemployment benefits (up to 90 percent of the last wage earned, for more than 4 years), but it has in place mechanisms for monitoring the unemployed that allow an efficient return to employment. At the other extreme, the Netherlands attains full employment with a turnover rate as weak as France, but, unlike France, manages wage formation in a flexible manner, thanks to unions that are prepared to make compromises adapted to the macroeconomic context.

Chapter 3

Age Structure

Nothing better illustrates the differences highlighted by Esping-Andersen than an analysis of the employment market in age terms.[7] To simplify the presentation, I limit the comparison here to France and the United States. (See tables 3.3–3.5.)

Let us take the employment rate for those aged 25–54 years first. It is equivalent in France and the United States. If the French system of labor contracts really worked as badly as some think, causing an attrition of job seekers on the labor market, that ought to lead to less employ-

Table 3.3
Rates of employment by age (men and women).

	15–64	15–24	25–54	55–64
France	62.3	26	79.6	40.7
US	71.5	53.9	79.3	60.8

Table 3.4
Rates of employment by age (men).

	15–64	15–24	25–54	55–64
France	67.8	29.3	86.6	43.8
US	77.6	55.2	86.9	67.0

Table 3.5
Rates of employment by age (women).

	15–64	15–24	25–54	55–64
France	56.9	29.6	80.7	40.2
US	65.6	58.6	75.3	57.0

ment in the central age range of 25–54, both for men and for women. In the canonical model of the labor market,[8] for example, the various frictions introduced by an inefficient labor market depress employment across all categories of workers. The fact that persons aged 25–54 work as much in the United States as in France poses a specific challenge to these models.

Likewise, the fact that French women aged 25–54 actually work more than American women casts doubt on the hypothesis that high taxation is a disincentive to work. Women generally exhibit a higher elasticity of the supply of labor to income and taxation. The explanation of this apparent paradox is in fact straightforward: taxes make it possible to pay for the day care that makes it possible for mothers to work. This is also what explains the high labor-force participation of Swedish women.

Now let us turn to youth unemployment. In France, since the end of the 1970s, there have existed two kinds of labor contract. The open-ended one (the *contrat à durée indéterminée*, or CDI) makes it difficult to fire or lay off those covered by it. The time-limited one (the *contrat à durée déterminée*, or CDD) is offered to new entrants; it specifies a fixed period (generally a year), at the conclusion of which the worker may either gain access to a CDI or be let go. The CDD contributes significantly to youth unemployment, since it forces them into an artificially high rate of turnover. As the economists Olivier Blanchard and Augustin Landier show,[9] a French employer too often prefers to let a young worker go at the termination of his CDD rather than transform it into a CDI, because of a rational anticipation that the worker will modify his wage demands once the changeover has been made. Far from representing an acceptable compromise, the CDD produces the worst possible outcome for a young worker: high turnover, American style, and low rates of hiring, European style.

Unemployment among seniors is the other cause of French underemployment. Here France displays a marked imbalance with the United States. For workers aged 55–64, the rate of employment is 47 percent for men in France, whereas it is 70 percent in the United States. For women, the figure is 40 percent in France, versus 57 percent in the United States. This lopsidedness is intimately bound up with a major factor: the lowering of the age of retirement that was introduced in France in the 1980s in order to "fight unemployment." Research clearly establishes that the unemployment of seniors in France is principally explained by this factor, through comparison with its level 30 years ago, or the levels found in other countries. It is not the biological age of persons that explains their underemployment, but their social age—the time they have left to work before taking retirement.[10]

The two extremes of underemployment among young people and seniors illustrate the pathologies of the French model. It is corporatist and Mediterranean at the same time—corporatist in that it creates two unequal statuses among workers (those on CDD and those on CDI), Mediterranean in its focus on protecting the position of adults aged 25–55 (to the detriment of other segments of the population). Cultural idiosyncrasies do translate into policy choices, although somehow unconsciously.[11]

The Americanization of France

It is always risky to view one country or another as a static entity. In the previous chapter, I noted how demographic changes are shaped by television. Within Europe, Margaret Thatcher's United Kingdom was quite different from the UK of the post–World War II Labour governments. Denmark is another example—frequently and understandably commented on—of a country that was able (belatedly, during the 1990s) to find an original path between Anglo American flexibility and Scandinavian solidarity. The United States too is constantly being reinvented. The comparison between the 1960s and the 1980s is no simpler there than it is in Europe.

It is nevertheless tempting to see the American model as a variant of what Esping-Andersen calls the liberal welfare state. Weak regulation of the labor market reflects the aspiration to leave this market as free as possible, in conformity with the British philosophical underpinnings described by d'Iribarne.. But the United States also embodies a variant of the German model. Americans are often proud to belong to a community—American churches, for example, which seem so bizarre from a French perspective, and whose importance Tocqueville noted, reveal a "German" aspect of American society.

There is one factor, though, that silently and power-
fully plays a role in the explanation of American specific-
ity: the racial question. In an analysis of the functioning
of the American labor market, Gavin Wright and Warren
Whatley have shown that American distrust of rigid "labor
contracts" has to be understood in relation to the need to
leave the age of slavery behind.[12] Every long-term contract
is suspect because it evokes the bond of indefinite subor-
dination of the slave. This point of view is evidently very
close to the interpretation given by Philippe d'Iribarne of
the English definition of liberty: a free man is one who is
no other man's slave. Alberto Alesina, Edward Glaeser,
and Bruce Sacerdote have likewise shown very convinc-
ingly that Americans often confound the social question
and the racial question.[13] When asked "Why are poor
people poor?" two-thirds of Americans respond that it is
because they are lazy and only one-third that they have
been unlucky. The proportion is exactly reversed when
the same question is put to Americans who "have recently
dined with an African-American friend." The authors
show the considerable weight of the racial question in the
evolution of the American welfare state. The idea that the
welfare state is less developed in the United States because
Americans are more individualistic than Europeans is con-
tradicted by a host of statistics. The number of Americans
who make charitable donations is three times greater
than the comparable number of Europeans, and the
average amount donated is more than ten times greater.
But since in the United States the social question is over-

laid with a racial question, the poor man is not seen as an unfortunate brother. So social policy in American states is always inversely correlated to the number of African-Americans inhabiting that state. This is not yet the case with Europeans, the majority of whom continue to think (according to the same survey) that a poor person is like everyone else except that he has had bad luck.

The Youth of the Outer Suburbs

It is possible, however, that today Europe in general and France in particular are simply in the middle of Americanizing their conception of poverty. Considerable gaps have already opened up between rates of poverty among "whites" and those of "minorities."

A spectacular example of this French failure of integra tion occurred in the summer of 2005. France was shaken by a revolt in the *banlieues* of the same order of magni tude as the one that Los Angeles experienced in 1992. This revolt illustrates the failure of the French model of integration. The youth in the *banlieues* suffer in the first place from a pathologically high rate of unemployment. The unemployment rate for the whole population of labor-market participants is 10 percent, that for young people 20 percent, and that for young people in the *cités* 40 percent. French unemployment follows the clear gra-dient that I highlighted above: there is strong protection for those who have succeeded in acquiring seniority (the "insiders") and weak protection for those who have not (the "outsiders"). In this respect France is perfectly representative of the neo-corporatist compromises that Esping-Andersen describes.

What makes French unemployment (up to a point, at least) socially tolerable for the young workers is the simple assumption that young outsiders are likely to become adult insiders sooner or later. The problem is that, in the meantime, young people are not all "lodged at the same inn," to use an idiomatic French expression. The fact is, while they wait to find a stable job, young people have to live off adults. We see the characteristics of Mediterranean capitalism as defined by Bruno Amable: it is family solidarity that enables the system to function.

This is the crux of the problem in the French *banlieues*. If unemployment is at the limit of what is acceptable for the population in general, it is catastrophic for the populations at risk. The central paradox, which is poorly understood in much talk about the *banlieues*, is this: young people in the *cités* are deprived of the intra-familial solidarity that makes the "French model" tolerable for other young people. There is a stereotype to the effect that strong identification with their own communities leads these young people to "exclude" themselves from the rest of society in favor of their own communities. But the truth is almost opposite: the social existence of young people in the *banlieues* is fragile because of weak community ties.

The American example reveals that the integration of minorities is a function of the strength of intra-community solidarity. When the Cubans driven out by Fidel Castro in 1980 had to look for work in Miami, more than half of them found it in a Cuban-American enterprise (where they were still working 10 years later). When communities are close-knit (as Chinese communities are, for example), the new arrival can also count on a community credit mechanism, which functions like the African *tontines*: the first to repay aids in the financing of those who follow. Thus primitive accumulation can occur, offering the second and then third generations the resources that will permit them real integration.[11] Why are certain communities weak and others strong? Those who would look for the answer in the original ethos of the community itself must explain why Mexicans fail where Cubans succeed, despite their common background as Catholics and Spanish-Americans. Often immigrant communities succeed even when their country of origin is in crisis. What is certain is that the United States does not regard such community self-help as objectionable, and even encourages it.[15]

The French model, with its total commitment to republican meritocracy, is allergic to the idea that strong intra-community bonds may promote integration. It prefers to concentrate on the fact that when the educational level of parents is low, the handicap rapidly becomes insurmountable for their children. This line of reasoning is irrefutable, but it is incomplete. In developing countries too, the educational handicap of parents is crushing. That does not prevent certain ones from making up the initial lag, sometimes in two or three generations. Singapore was 90 percent illiterate at the end of World War II; today it is a world leader, ranking ahead of France. But unlike the school system in Singapore, where children benefit from programs deliberately tailored to their level, France's republican system sets a norm corresponding to the national average, which is poorly adapted to children residing in the *banlieues*.

France, in selecting its elites from the melting pot of republican schooling, wants to believe that the latter is open to all—thus illustrating both the social hypocrisy and the ignorance of itself emphasized by d'Iribarne. In result, it has great difficulty in thinking through the inequality that in fact separates the different participants in this meritocratic race. To conceive—sometimes even to let itself conceive—ways of offsetting this is very hard for France. In the belief that it is fighting poverty, France has actually allowed it to take on the profile seen in the United States. Poverty has become ghettoized. Third- or fourth-generation offspring of families from North Africa find themselves trapped in poverty that stigmatizes them socially and confines them to *banlieues* from which it is hard to escape. The rise of the extreme right, whose candidate in the presidential elections of 2005 beat out the sitting prime minister in the first round of voting, illustrates what we may call the Americanization of France: the tendency to think that the poor are so by nature, not by accident. Aristotle once said the same thing about slaves.

The Case for a European University

European diversity proves that it would be futile to associate the post-industrial age with any single form of social solidarity. In fact, it is tempting to conclude that the range of variations has increased in Europe: as though, faced with the transformation of the 1970s and the 1980s, each country had had to draw upon its own national character to find a response. One could simply speak of an industrial society, with very similar blue collars, managers and unions. It is much more difficult to speak of a model of the post-industrial society. Local and global considerations get matched in many idiosyncratic ways across countries. We return to this theme in the general conclusion.

The fact that no single European social model exists need not be in itself a source of concern. If we regard a social model as a way of ensuring the mutualization of social risks within a given community, nothing entails that the same structure of solidarity must prevail across the whole continent. Yet it is pertinent to raise the question of a European social model, since it leads to the deeper question of the significance of the European Union. What remains of the ambition of Europe's pioneers to bring into being a European people, capable one day of forging the "United States of Europe" of which Victor Hugo dreamed? It is putting it mildly to state that Europe today is struggling to understand its own identity. The Europe of Dante and Cervantes, of Diderot and Goethe, is a fine idea in theory, but its practical consequence is thin. The European languages, apart from English, are rarely spoken outside their home countries. The countries of Europe are today much more impervious to one another than they were in the Middle Ages, when the Catholic Church provided a single focus of attachment and a common language.

Underlying this divergence between medieval and contemporary Europe is a simple factor: there is no European university system in whose lecture halls the youth of Europe could learn to know and appreciate one another. This question leads back to the definition of the post-industrial economy sketched above. A post-industrial economy is actually the union of two opposing terms: the world of images and ideas, which are globalized, and the world of direct relationships, of F2F, which are localized. Out of the former, a universal consciousness may arise. The latter, in contrast, makes national peculiarities more profound. Lacking a European university system, Europe fails twice: once at participating efficiently to the creation of world knowledge, and once at creating a "European people" that might, quite simply, gets to know each other.

Apart from its cultural aspect, this absence weighs heavily on European competitiveness. Every year, the University of Shanghai publishes a ranked list of the top 500 universities in the world. Of the top ten in the ranking for 2005, only Cambridge and Oxford (second and ninth respectively) are not located in the United States.[16] Of the top 100, only five are German, four French, and one

Italian. Like all rankings, the University of Shanghai's is debatable. It tends to ignore publications by researchers attached to external research bodies, and awards a premium to large establishments over smaller ones. The École Normale Supérieure, although it garnered all the Fields medals (the highest distinction in mathematics) awarded to France, appears in 93rd place, because its size and the difficulty of identifying its teaching faculty reduce its visibility. The power (intellectual and financial) of the American universities is, however, obvious. Not taking seriously this ranking because it is not perfect would be to behave like an ostrich.

Should Europeans copy the American model? The blunt response is "Why not?" The twentieth century was dominated by a practically universal mode of organizing work "scientifically": Taylorism. If we assume that scientific and technical innovation will be to the twenty-first century what the organization of industrial labor was to the twentieth, it is not far-fetched to take the view that a "scientific organization of knowledge" is equally necessary. The university is to the new century what the Fordist firm was to the previous one: the institution that determines the raw materials—knowledge and training—that feed into the rest of society.

As sites of the production of knowledge, the American universities owe their effectiveness to the fact that they supply an answer to the major contradictions inherent in the production of knowledge: the trade-off between competition and cooperation, and that between

fundamental and applied research. The American universities are undeniably competitive. They compete for the
best students and the best teachers, they enjoy a financial
autonomy that comes from high tuition fees and their
independent endowments. They are also a site of cooperation: faculty members move from one university to
another freely, thanks to seminars and sabbatical years,
and they combine to present research proposals to the
National Science Foundation. But above all, the American
universities are strong enough to engage in dialogue
on equal terms with other centers of power in society,
whether political or industrial. It is here that the highly
controversial question of the relation between fundamental and applied research plays out.

French researchers have recently manifested their fear
of seeing their research agendas dictated by an industrial
or bureaucratic logic. Echoing their disquiet, the presi-
dent of the French Academy of Science, Edouard Brézin,
remarked that electricity was not discovered while search-
ing for a new way to make candles. By that he meant,
and rightly, that the logic of scientific discoveries is not
reducible to the uses expected from them. Nevertheless,
it would be wrong to end the debate with that observation. The extreme idea that science and technology form
two worlds hermetically sealed off from one another is
equally false. The economic historian Joel Mokyr notes
that thermodynamics was born in the nineteenth century
from research aimed at improving the efficiency of steam
engines.[17] The new dialectic between science and technol-

ogy is, according to Mokyr, the crucial factor that explains why the industrial revolution of the eighteenth century differed from those that preceded it.

It is because the links between fundamental and applied research are complex that it is indispensable to have powerful and autonomous institutions that will protect researchers from the short-termism of industry without going to the other extreme of ignoring the social demands addressed to them. The fact that American universities are teaching centers plays a decisive role in this respect. To have to meet the demand for intellectual training is a powerful stimulus, compelling them to address themselves to the long-term trends of society without having to renounce the imperatives of science.

Even apart from the level of expenditure, European research remains in actuality a stack of national research programs that is worth less in total than the sum of the individual parts. The procedures for allocating EU resources, which are very careful to respect the equilibria among member nations, are unable to bring into being centers of excellence comparable to those that spring up in the United States around the best universities. No one would accept it if the EU tried to direct a stream of resources of the kind one observes around Boston or San Francisco toward Oxford or Bologna. Nor is the role played by the US Department of Defense transferable to the European context.

Will Europeans be able to create a system of universities that does justice to their history and their diversity, but that also has the capacity to bring Europe into the knowledge economy? We have to hope so, but there is no guarantee. According to Joel Mokyr, the decline of Britain in the nineteenth century derived in part from its incapacity to create engineering schools, like those founded contemporaneously in France and Germany, that would have permitted the children and grandchildren of the inventors of the steam engine and the spinning jenny to build on the innovations of their forefathers. Mokyr portrays the worthy descendants of these inventor-geniuses enrolling instead in "public" (that is, private) schools, in order to study the arts of domesticity or good taste, thus separating Britain, at the dawn of the twentieth century, from the great innovations (e.g., the internal-combustion engine and the electric motor) that were about to reshape the world. Britain's handicap of yesterday has become Europe's handicap of today.

Conclusion

Europe has proved that it is possible to go from war to peace in the space of a few years. It has proved that economic integration could preserve cultural diversity. The European Commission has invented a new model for the construction of supranational institutions that respect the sovereignty of states. But Europe is discovering belatedly that the creation of a single market is not enough to create a shared citizenship, and that face-to-face contact among Europeans is also necessary. Here is where the project to create a European university system takes on major importance. By frequenting the same lecture halls, the students would not just be helping to equip Europe for the knowledge society. They would also be planting the seeds of a moral and affective community. It is possible that the Erasmus Program, which allows European students to study in other European countries, will be to the Europe of the future what the coal and steel community was to the common market, the euro, and the EU: the small beginning of a long march that may shape Europe's destiny in the twenty-first century.

Conclusion
The New Social
Question

No longer is the factory, as it once was, a place where workers, foremen, engineers, and owners mingled socially. Their relations were conflictual, of course, but each could directly measure his dependence on the others. Today the engineers are in research bureaus, the maintenance jobs are with a service company, and the industrial jobs have been contracted out, robotized, or moved offshore. The factories have been hollowed out: the jobs are elsewhere, and people no longer get to meet one another.

Not so long ago, in a normally constituted city, the rich dwelt on second floors and the poor on top floors. Rich and poor encountered one another on staircases. Even if they did not speak to one another, their children sometimes went to the same school. Since elevators have come into widespread use, residential buildings are occupied by the rich or by the poor, but never by both at once. Rich and poor now live in separate districts. The neighborhood has ceased to be a site of social mixing. Worse still, with subways the outer suburbs tend to get pushed farther away from the fashionable part of town. Not so long ago, the workers' residential quarters were close to the city center, because they had to walk to work. With the subway, the distance could increase. The residents of the *banlieues* now travel in to the city center on Saturday night to get their fill of images, then go back home. The "problem" housing projects are only the visible tip of a much vaster process in which each social group sees the next social stratum up, to which it was once adjacent, drifting away. As the French sociologist Jacques Donzelot has noted, in the United States gated communities are arising in which the rich can seclude themselves. The French economist Eric Maurin has shown meticulously to what extent France's social classes are sealing themselves off through endogamy.[1] A series of closed worlds is being formed, with not much more in common than the images from the "problem" neighborhoods that flash onto their television screens. And the only social demand is the demand for public security.

Assortative Mating

Some light is shed on this propensity for social endogamy by the theory of assortative mating.[2] The University of Chicago economist Gary Becker, a professor at Chicago and Nobel laureate in economics, proposed this theory in his iconoclastic research on the economic analysis of marriage. It perfectly illustrates the forces that play out when society is left to itself. Becker's theory goes like this: When a man and a woman are each seeking a marriage partner, two kinds of mating (or "pairing") are possible. In the first, a man who is good-looking and rich marries a woman who is also good-looking and rich. In this hypothesis, those best endowed marry among themselves, and by doing so they set off a shock wave that propagates through the marriage market. For if the best endowed marry among themselves, those less endowed will have no other choice but to do the same, since there will be no more really good-looking and very rich people left to marry. The same constraint works its way down the social chain, forming a pattern in which each stratum of society closes itself off to those living just beneath it.

Becker shows, however, that another sequence is possible: one that leads to asymmetric pairings. It is logically possible to envision a marriage between an unprepossessing poor man and a beautiful rich woman. Why? In everyday language, we would say "because he is nice" (or kind, or sweet). In Becker's terms, the reasoning is as follows: A marriage is both a pooling of resources (time, affect, money) and a rule for sharing them out. In the case of a symmetric marriage, only one share-out rule is possible: that of parity. If two equally endowed persons marry, the concessions to be made will be equally distributed. But an unprepossessing man may quite possibly convince a beautiful woman that he will be more faithful than a handsome man, precisely because he has nothing else to offer. To say of an unprepossessing man that he is "nice" signifies, in economic terms, that he accepts a share-out rule more favorable to his partner (except if she is equally nice, in which case we are dealing with a natural trait they have in common). The share-out rules can transform the logic of marriage, and can create an asymmetric pairing.

Within the framework of this strange theory, we can interpret industrial society as an asymmetric marriage between highly endowed people (engineers) and less well-endowed ones (workers). The engineers gain from this arrangement if the workers are "nice." When the workers become too demanding, the asymmetric pairing gets broken. The turn of the 1960s was the moment of this divorce, when the aspirations of workers and young people exacerbated the contradictions of Fordism. The union of opposites that had come about in the Fordist factory ceased to be socially pertinent. And so we pass over into another logic: that of assortative pairing, which puts an end to the previous exogamy. Those best endowed decide to remain among themselves. Those just below, in frustration, close off access to the level below them in turn. The secession of the richest reverberates down through the whole of society. Endogamy becomes the rule. The theory of assortative pairings throws into relief an important point: people find themselves grouped together, in homogeneous social classes, less out of self-love than out of rejection of the other, of those who are poorer.

Politics, Economics, and Society

In *A New Paradigm for Understanding Today's World,*[3] the
French sociologist Alain Touraine sums up the evolution of the relations between politics, economics, and
the social sphere in a way that illuminates the place this
new age of social segregation occupies in the long history
of the European nations. His point of departure is the
start of the second millennium. Around the twelfth and
thirteenth centuries CE, political power gradually liberated itself from religious power. It was the age when the
king of France surrounded himself with legal experts
who helped him to delimit the area of his own sovereignty, separate from that of the Church. Freed of religious tutorship, political power subsequently made an
alliance with economic power. This was the mercantilist
moment. In response to Machiavelli, who thought that
the prince must be rich and his subjects poor, the mercan-
tilists wished to prove that the two went together. In their
eyes, princes and merchants had converging interests,
the wealth of the latter feeding the treasury of the former.
Subsequently the economy liberated itself in turn from
politics. This was the era of laissez-faire in the nineteenth
century. The economy freed itself from the tutorship
of the state and claimed autonomy. This was the "great
transformation" in which the long-established European
nations all became market economies.

Economic laissez-faire had led to considerable human
distress in the first half of the nineteenth century. Working-

class poverty undermined the foundations of the market economy, which initially proved incapable of ensuring the well-being of workers. It is from this period of social tensions emerged the various figures of social solidarity which Esping-Andersen has studied. Still, it was really with Fordism that industrial society blossomed, creating new forms of social solidarity, of exogamy, within the firms themselves.

We have now entered a new epoch, in which social cohesion and economic forces are splitting apart. The rich are seceding, clustering according to the logic of assortative pairing, obliging those beneath them to follow suit.

The consequences of this social segregation are not primarily measured in economic terms. The source of economic growth has moved: it now flows much more from research laboratories than from factories. Like the Internet, physical production easily follows the line of least resistance, and is able to evade the various blockages it encounters. It is not the economic realm that suffers: it is society, which no longer understands itself, and tries to interpret itself in cultural or religious terms.

The Real and the Imaginary

Left to itself, society needs nourishment from collective identities, and it is here that the reasoning of Alain Touraine may be taken further. Over and above aspects specific to France, the crisis of the *banlieues* is perfectly emblematic of the new social question in general, includ-

ing the way its origins are disguised. Community identification is on the rise everywhere, but it is not the
explanatory factor some take it for. It is the consequence
rather than the cause of social segregation. In a sense,
things may have come full circle: the religious realm is
engaged in forging a new alliance with the social. Religion
becomes an answer to social solitude. Everyone is
attempting, in his or her own way, to bridge the growing
divide between the virtual world and the real world.

By analogy with the sequence proposed by Touraine,
the central problem is once again, as it was at the start of
the second millennium, to bring about, to re-invent, "laic"
institutions, meaning institutions that are not pre-empted
by social and cultural relations. To rethink trade union-
ism and the universities, to think through world governance on one hand and the governance of cities and local
collectivities on the other, has become just as important as
carrying on with the classic functions of the regalian state
(public order, justice, military defense). For each of these
institutions, the task is the same: to build a social infrastructure that will help persons and countries to live out
a destiny worthy of their expectations, that will release
them from the paradox of living in a real world that is too
poor and a virtual world that is too rich.

Notes

Introduction

1. Let us avoid a misunderstanding at the outset: industrial work never bulked larger in quantitative terms than other forms of work in the US or France; the only "industrial" country where it did so, briefly, was the UK. But the organization of work that came into being in industry rapidly influenced other sectors (see chapter 1 below).

2. See Peter Gottschalk and Robert Moffitt, "The Growth of Earning Instability in the US Labor Market," *Brookings Papers on Economic Activity* 2 (1994); Adriaan Kalwij and Rob Alessie, "Permanent and Transitory Wages of British Men, 1975 2001: Year, Age, and Cohort Effects," *Journal of Applied Econometrics* 22, no. 6 (2007): 1063–1093. According to these studies, more than half of the increase in wage inequality in the US and the UK could be explained by the rise in the variability of workers' income.

3. Colin Clark, *The Conditions of Economic Progress* (Macmillan, 1939); Jean Fourastié, *Le grand espoir du XXe siècle* (Presses universitaires de France, 1949).

4. Philippe Askenazy, "Innovative Workplace Practices and Occupational Health and Safety in the United States," *Industrial and Economic Democracy* 22, no. 4 (2001): 485–516.

5. Daniel Bell, *The Coming of Post-Industrial Society* (Harper, 1973).

6. On this point, see Olivier Mongin, "Puissance du virtuel, déchaînements des possibles et dévalorisation du monde. Retour sur des

remarques de Jean-Toussaint Desanti," *Esprit*, August 2004, available at http://www.esprit.presse.fr.

7. Emile Durkheim, *La division du travail social* (Presses Universitaires de France, 1991, in the series "Quadrige"). Published in English as *The Division of Labor in Society* (Free Press, 1984).

Chapter 1

1. This term is borrowed from the title of Karl Polanyi's book *The Great Transformation: The Political and Economic Origins of Our Time* (Beacon, 2001; first published in 1944).

2. See Elhanan Helpman et al., *General Purpose Technologies and Economic Growth* (MIT Press, 1998).

3. Cited in François Caron, *Les deux révolutions industrielles du XXe siècle* (Albin Michel, 1997).

4. Ford was overtaken by General Motors because Alfred P. Sloan, the head of GM, was the first to grasp the need to diversify his product line, and organize the firm to that end. But Sloan never envisaged authorizing workers to interrupt the assembly line in order to reprogram the colors of the cars.

5. Michael Piore and Charles Sabel, *The Second Industrial Divide* (Basic Books, 1984).

6. See Askenazy, "Innovative Workplace Practices and Occupational Health and Safety in the United States."

7. Mark Shapiro and Joseph Stiglitz, "Equilibrium Unemployment as a Worker Discipline Device," *American Economic Review* 74 (1984): 433–444.

8. Henri Weber, *Que reste-t-il de Mai 68?* in the collection *Points* (Seuil, 1998).

9. Louis Dumont, *Homo aequalis. Genèse et épanouissement de l'idéologie économique* (Gallimard, 1977).

10. See Manuel Castells, *The Rise of the Network Society*, second edition (Blackwell, 2000).

11. Unix was developed by Bell Laboratories. An FCC investigation of their monopoly power forced them to put it into the public domain, and from then on it was developed by university researchers.

12. Raghu Rajan and Luigi Zingales, "The Great Reversals: The Politics of Financial Development in the 20th Century," *Journal of Financial Economics* 69, no. 1 (2003): 5–50.

13. Adolf A. Berle, Jr. and Gardiner C. Means, *Modern Corporation and Private Property* (Harcourt, 1932).

14. Xavier Gabaix and Augustin Landier, in "Why Has CEO Pay Increased So Much?" (working paper 06-13, MIT Department of Economics, 2006; available at http://ssrn.com), show that heads of companies profit from a rarity rent. Since they can accept the highest bid offered, they obtain a remuneration in proportion not just to the market capitalization of their own firm, but to the growth of the stock market in general.

15. Andrei Shleifer and Lawrence H. Summers, "Breach of Trust in Hostile Takeovers," in *Corporate Takeovers: Causes and Consequences*, ed. A. Auerbach (University of Chicago Press, 1988).

16. Richard S. Ruback and Michael C. Jensen, "The Market for Corporate Control: The Scientific Evidence," *Journal of Financial Economics* 11 (1983): 5–50; available at http://ssrn.com.

17. Quoted from an article by Robert Solow in *New York Times Book Review*, July 12, 1987.

18. Arthur M. Okun, *Prices and Quantities: A Macroeconomic Analysis* (Brookings Institution, 1981). For a similar idea, applied to international trade, see Marianne Bertrand, From the Invisible Handshake to the Invisible Hand? How Import Competition Changes the Employment Relationship, NBER working paper W6900, 1999, available at http://ssrn.com.

19. In the US and the UK, it is not jobs that are threatened, or that become more volatile: it is the remuneration of employees. In France, it is the reverse.

20. Luc Boltanski and Eve Chiappello, *Le nouvel esprit du capitalisme* (Gallimard, 1999).

Chapter 2

1. Raymond Aron, *Dix-huit leçons sur la société industrielle* (Gallimard, 1962); in English, *Eighteen Lectures on Industrial Society* (Weidenfeld and Nicolson, 1967). The present work is inspired by Aron.

2. Kevin O'Rourke and John Williamson, *Globalization and History: The Evolution of a Nineteenth-Century Atlantic Economy* (MIT Press, 1999).

3. We are in a paradoxical situation today, since, with the Chinese surplus helping to finance the American deficit, it is the great power itself that is being financed by developing countries.

4. Daron Acemoglu, Simon Johnson, and James Robinson, "The Colonial Origins of Comparative Development: An Empirical Investigation," *American Economic Review* 91 (2001): 1369–1401.

5. This is according to the figures of Angus Maddison, *The World Economy*, volume 1, *A Millennial Perspective* (2001), published by the OECD Development Centre. (Volume 2, *Historical Statistics*, was published in 2003. The OECD has a dedicated website for these books: http://www.theworldeconomy.org/.) Maddison revises the figures given by Paul Bairoch, which showed smaller differences in 1820.

6. According to Maddison's data, the income of a Chinese person was 1/14 that of a British person in 1973, 3 years before the death of Mao. It was 1/3 that of a British person in 1820, and 1/9 in 1913.

7. Here I follow Paul Krugman and Tony Venables, "Globalization and the Inequality of Nations," *Quarterly Journal of Economics* 110 (1995): 857–880.

8. Robert Feenstra, "Integration of Trade and Disintegration of Production in the Global Economy," *Journal of Economic Perspectives* 12, no. 4 (1998): 31–50.

9. See Eric Maurin, David Thesmar, and Mathias Thoenig, "Globalization and the Demand for Skill: An Export Based Channel," CEPR discussion paper 3406, 2002; available at http://ssrn.com. They show that firms that participate in international trade tend to reduce their activity as manufacturers in the strict sense, and shift their focus to management and commercial development.

10. Gary Becker, *A Treatise on the Family*, enlarged edition (Harvard University Press, 1991; first published in 1981).

11. Demographers who prefer the history of mentalities to that of material progress find reinforcement for their hypotheses here. See Hervé le Bras and Emmanuel Todd, *L'invention de la France* (Hachette, 1981). It remains an open question, however, why the today's demographic shift is occurring simultaneously in so many countries.

12. Jacques Delors and Kemal Dervis have proposed the creation of a Council of Economic Security, charged with nominating the directors of the large international agencies and ensuring that the norms produced by the World Trade Organization on one hand, and the World Health Organization, the International Labor Organization, and a new agency for ecology on the other, are balanced. See Kemal Dervis, *A Better Globalization: Legitimacy, Governance and Reform* (Brookings Institution Press, 2005).

13. Philippe Martin, Thierry Mayer, and Mathias Thoenig, Make Trade, Not War? CEPR discussion paper 5218, 2005; available at http://ssrn com. The authors show that bilateral trade does indeed reduce conflictuality between two nations, but with the risk of increasing it with others.

14. Even if the terrorists themselves are not poor: they come primarily from the educated classes. See Alan B. Krueger and Jitka Maleckova, "Education, Poverty, Political Violence and Terrorism: Is There a Causal Connection?" NBER working paper W9074, 2002, last revised August 2004; available at http://ssrn.com.

Chapter 3

1. See Guy Debord, *La société du spectacle* (Buchet-Castel, 1967), published in English as *The Society of the Spectacle* (Zone Books, 1995). Debord was one of the "thinkers" of May 1968.

2. Philippe d'Iribarne, "Trois figures de la liberté," *Annales: Histoire, Sciences Sociales* 58, no. 5 (2003): 953–980.

3. Michel Albert, *Capitalisme contre capitalisme* (Seuil, 1991); in English, *Capitalism vs. Capitalism: How America's Obsession with Individual*

Achievement and Short-Term Profit Has Led It to the Brink of Collapse (Four Walls Eight Windows, 1993).

4. Bruno Amable, *Les cinq capitalismes: Diversité des systèmes économiques et sociaux dans la mondialisation* (Seuil, 2005). The last type of capitalism reviewed by Amable is Asiatic capitalism, centered on loyalty to the firm.

5. Olivier Blanchard and Justin Wolfers, "The Role of Shocks and Institutions in the Rise of European Unemployment: The Aggregate Evidence," *Economic Journal* 110, no. 462 (2000): 1–33.

6. For a survey, see Olivier Blanchard, "European Unemployment: The Evolution of Facts and Ideas," *Economic Policy* 21, no. 45 (2006): 5–59.

7. See Guiseppe Bertola, Francine D. Blau, and Lawrence M. Kahn, "Labor Market Institutions and Demographic Employment Patterns," *Journal of Population Economics* 20 (2007): 833–867.

8. Christopher A. Pissarides and Dale T. Mortensen, "Symposium: Search and Matching Models of Unemployment," *Review of Economic Studies* 61, no. 3 (1994): 397–415.

9. Olivier Blanchard and Augustin Landier, "The Perverse Effects of Partial Labour Market Reform: Fixed-Term Contracts in France," *Economic Journal* 112, no. 480 (2002): F214–F244.

10. See Antoine d'Autume, Jean-Paul Betbèze, and Jean-Olivier Hairault, Les seniors et l'emploi en France, Rapports du Conseil d'analyse économique no. 58 (La documentation française, 2006); available at http://www.ladocumentationfrancaise.fr.

11. For an introduction to the booming literature, see Yann Algan and Pierre Cahuc, "Social attitudes and Macroeconomic performance: An epidemiological approach, CEPR working paper 2007. See also Guido Tabellini, "Institutions and Culture," Presidential Lecture given at the EEA meetings in Budapest, 2007.

12. Gavin Wright and Warren Whatley, "Race, Human Capital and Labour Markets in American History," in *Labour Market Evolution: The Economic History of Market Integration, Wage Flexibility, and the Employment Relation*, ed. G. Grantham and M. MacKinnon (Routledge, 1994).

13. Alberto F. Alesina, Edward L. Glaeser, and Bruce Sacerdote, "Why Doesn't the US Have a European-style Welfare State?" Discussion paper 1933, Harvard Institute of Economic Research, 2001, available at http://ssrn.com.

14. This idea is connected to that contained in the notion of "social capital" explored by the American political scientist Robert Putnam.

15. In Philippe d'Iribarne's terms, the US actually embodies a compromise between British and German values. Freedom of contract is essential, but so are communities, congregations, and so on: another example of blending.

16. Luc Bronner, "Recherche: les universités françaises réalisent des performances mitigées," Le Monde, August 23, 2005. The ranking for 2005, and the ones for earlier and subsequent years, are available at http://ed.sjtu.edu.

17. Joel Mokyr, The Gifts of Athena: Historical Origins of the Knowledge Economy (Princeton University Press, 2002).

Conclusion

1. Eric Maurin, Le Ghetto Français (Seuil/République des Idées, 2005); Jacques Donzelot, Faire société: la politique de la ville aux États-Unis et en France (Seuil, 2003).

2. Gary Becker, A Treatise on the Family, enlarged edition (Harvard University Press, 1991; first published in 1981). See also Daniel Cohen, Richesse du monde, pauvretés des nations (Flammarion, 1997), published in English as The Wealth of the World and the Poverty of Nations (MIT Press, 1998).

3. Alain Touraine, Un nouveau paradigme (Fayard, 2005), published in English as A New Paradigm for Understanding Today's World (Polity, 2007).

Index